THE ENTREPRENEURSHIP SERIES

Management for Entrepreneurs

SECOND EDITION

Other books in the series:
Entrepreneurship and How to Establish Your Own Business
Basic Financial Management for Entrepreneurs
Marketing for Entrepreneurs
Computing for a Small Business
Entrepreneurial Skills
Human Resource Management
The Franchise Option – How to Franchise Your Business

THE ENTREPRENEURSHIP SERIES

Management for Entrepreneurs
SECOND EDITION

Andreas de Beer
Alba Kritzinger
Nina Venter
Jan Steyn
Madeleine Labuschagne
Edmund Ferreira
Darelle Groenewald
Jo Stapelberg

Consulting Editor: Cecile Nieuwenhuizen

Series Co-ordinating Editor: Cecile Nieuwenhuizen

JUTA

First published in 1996 as *Management of a Small Business*
Reprinted 1997
Reprinted 1998
Second edition published as *Management for Entrepreneurs*, 2002
Reprinted 2003
Reprinted 2004
Reprinted June 2006
ISBN 0 7021 5543 8

© Juta & Co. Ltd, 2002
P.O. Box 24309, Lansdowne 7779

This book is copyright under the Berne Convention. In terms of the Copyright Act 98 of 1978 no part of this book may be reproduced or transmitted in any form or by any means, electronic or mechanical, including photocopying, recording or by any information storage and retrieval system, without permission in writing from the publisher.

Project manager (CCDD): Chris van Rooyen
Didactic advisor: Annemarie Bates
Editor (Afrikaans): Estelle van Rensburg
Editor (second edition): Alfred LeMaitre
Translators: Melanie Language, Keith Richmond
Illustrations: Mark Bates, Warren Nelson, André Plant
Icons: Carol Nelson
Cover design: Inspiration Sandwich
Book design and typesetting: Charlene Bate

Printed in South Africa by Mills Litho, Maitland, Cape Town

About the authors...

Andreas de Beer (Chapter 1) is a senior lecturer in the Department of Business Management at Technikon SA. He holds the degrees B.Com (Ed), B.Com (Hons), B.Ed and M.Ed. and has co-authored other books on management.

Nina Venter (Chapter 3) is National Registrar at a tertiary institute. She holds the degrees B.Com and B.Com (Hons) in Marketing and has co-authored another book on management.

Jan Steyn (Chapter 4) is a lecturer in Production Management and the acting executive director in the department of Logistics Management. He holds a M.Tech degree in Production Management and a diploma in Organisation and Work Study. He has co-authored other books on production management and supervisory management.

Madeleine Labuschagne (Chapter 5) is a lecturer in the Department of Business Management at the University of Pretoria. She holds the degrees B.Com, B.Com (Hons) and M.Com. She is also co-author of other books on business management, general management and small business management.

Edmund Ferreira (Chapter 6) is a senior lecturer in the Department of Business Management at Technikon SA. He holds the degrees B.Mil (Commercial Sciences), B.Com (Hons) in Manpower Management and M.Com (Business Management). He has co-authored other books on business management and office administration.

Darelle Groenewald (Chapter 7) is a senior lecturer in the Department of Business Management at RAU. She holds the degrees B.Com, B. Com (Hons) and M.Com (Business Management) and has co-authored other study material for Technical College certificates as well as other books on Business Management and Strategic Management.

Jo Stapelberg (Chapter 8) is a lecturer in Business Administration in the Department of Business Management at Technikon SA. She obtained her diploma in teaching as well as the degree B.Com at Unisa. She is also co-author of a book on business management.

Dr Cecile Nieuwenhuizen (Chapters 1 and 6) is a deputy chief lecturer in the Department of Business Management at Technikon SA. She holds the degrees BA (Comm), MBL and PhD (Criteria for the Financing of Small Industries) and a diploma in Small Business Management. She has co-authored other books on Strategic Management and Entrepreneurship and has presented entrepreneurship research papers at various international conferences. She has been involved in various small and medium enterprises as director and consultant. Cecile is the co-ordinating editor of the Entrepreneurship Series.

The late Alba Kritzinger (Chapter 2) was a senior lecturer in Credit Management in the Department of Business Management at Technikon SA. She attained the degrees B.Com, B.Com (Hons) (cum laude) and M.Com (Financial Management) at the University of Port Elizabeth.

CONTENTS

PREFACE xiii

KEY TO ICONS xiv

CHAPTER 1: GENERAL MANAGEMENT

1. LEARNING OBJECTIVES (OUTCOMES) 1
2. INTRODUCTION 1
3. THE MAIN MANAGEMENT FUNCTIONS 3
   - 3.1 Planning 3
   - 3.2 Organising 12
   - 3.3 Leadership 17
   - 3.4 Control 20
4. THE ADDITIONAL MANAGEMENT FUNCTIONS 23
   - 4.1 Coordination 23
   - 4.2 Decision-making 25
   - 4.3 Communication 25
   - 4.4 Motivation 25
   - 4.5 Delegation 25
   - 4.6 Discipline 25
5. SUMMARY 26
6. SELF-EVALUATION 26
7. REFERENCES 30

CHAPTER 2: THE FINANCIAL FUNCTION

1. LEARNING OBJECTIVES (OUTCOMES) 31
2. INTRODUCTION 31
3. FINANCIAL FUNCTION AND FINANCIAL MANAGEMENT 32
4. BASIC FINANCIAL CONCEPTS 34
5. OBJECTIVES OF FINANCIAL MANAGEMENT 41
6. TASKS OF FINANCIAL MANAGEMENT 49
7. SUMMARY 55
8. SELF-EVALUATION 55
9. REFERENCE 58

CHAPTER 3: THE MARKETING FUNCTION

1. LEARNING OBJECTIVES (OUTCOMES) 59
2. INTRODUCTION 59
3. THE MARKETING PROCESS 60
4. THE MARKETING PLAN 67
    - 4.1 Summary of the intended plan 68
    - 4.2 Current marketing situation 69
    - 4.3 Marketing analysis (SWOT analysis) 70
    - 4.4 Set objectives 71
    - 4.5 Marketing strategies (marketing mix) 72
    - 4.6 Action plan 74
    - 4.7 Budget 75
    - 4.8 Control 76
5. SUMMARY 77
6. SELF-EVALUATION 77
7. REFERENCES 81

CHAPTER 4: THE OPERATIONS FUNCTION

1. LEARNING OBJECTIVES (OUTCOMES) 82
2. INTRODUCTION 82
3. PRODUCTION MANAGEMENT VS. OPERATIONS MANAGEMENT 83
4. OPERATIONS MANAGEMENT IN THE TRANSFORMATION PROCESS 84
5. CAPACITY PLANNING 87
6. PRODUCTION SYSTEMS 90
   - 6.1 Job production 90
   - 6.2 Batch production 91
   - 6.3 Flow production 92
7. PRODUCT DESIGN 93
   - 7.1 Use or function 94
   - 7.2 Sales appearance 94
   - 7.3 Design effectiveness 94
   - 7.4 Raw materials 95
   - 7.5 Simplification 95
   - 7.6 Determining of costs 95
   - 7.7 Patents and patent law 95
   - 7.8 Consumer complaints 96
   - 7.9 Inquiries and after-sales service 96
8. PRODUCTION PLANNING 98
   - 8.1 Aggregate planning and master scheduling 98
   - 8.2 Operations scheduling 99
9. PROBLEM-SOLVING 102
10. SUMMARY 104
11. SELF-EVALUATION 104
12. REFERENCES 108

CHAPTER 5: THE PURCHASING FUNCTION

1. LEARNING OBJECTIVES (OUTCOMES) 109
2. INTRODUCTION 109
3. THE ROLE AND IMPORTANCE OF THE PURCHASING FUNCTION IN THE SMALL BUSINESS 110
4. OBJECTIVES OF THE PURCHASING FUNCTION 112
5. ACTIVITIES OF THE PURCHASING FUNCTION 120
6. MANAGEMENT OF THE PURCHASING FUNCTION 130
   - 6.1 Planning for purchasing 130
   - 6.2 Organising the purchasing function 133
   - 6.3 Controlling purchasing 136
7. SUMMARY 142
8. SELF-EVALUATION 143
9. REFERENCES 146

CHAPTER 6: THE HUMAN RESOURCE FUNCTION

1. LEARNING OBJECTIVES (OUTCOMES) 147
2. INTRODUCTION 147
3. JOB DESCRIPTION 148
4. JOB SPECIFICATION 150
5. HUMAN RESOURCE PLANNING 153
   - 5.1 Recruitment 154
   - 5.2 Selection 157
   - 5.3 Employment 160
   - 5.4 Induction 160
6. MOTIVATION 163
7. TRAINING AND DEVELOPMENT OF STAFF 164
8. REMUNERATION 166

9.	LABOUR RELATIONS	170
10.	OTHER FACTORS	172
11.	SUMMARY	173
12.	SELF-EVALUATION	173
13.	REFERENCES	175

CHAPTER 7: THE ADMINISTRATIVE FUNCTION

1.	LEARNING OBJECTIVES (OUTCOMES)		176
2.	INTRODUCTION		176
3.	INFORMATION MANAGEMENT AS A COMPONENT OF THE ADMINISTRATIVE FUNCTION		177
	3.1	Collection of data	179
	3.2	Processing of data	180
	3.3	Storing and retrieving	183
	3.4	Distribution of information	183
	3.5	Discarding of information	184
4.	THE INFORMATION NEEDS OF A BUSINESS		186
5.	ADMINISTRATIVE SYSTEMS		187
	5.1	Telephone system	188
	5.2	Postal mailing system	189
	5.3	Reprographic system (photocopying)	193
	5.4	Records management system	195
	5.5	Filing	195
	5.6	Filing of paper documents	197
	5.7	Mechanical filing	199
	5.8	Filing equipment	200
	5.9	Classifying and arranging of files	201
	5.10	Tips for effective filing	205
6.	FINANCIAL RECORD-KEEPING		206

7.	USE OF THE COMPUTER IN A SMALL BUSINESS	209
8.	SUMMARY	212
9.	SELF-EVALUATION	212
10.	REFERENCES	213

CHAPTER 8: THE PUBLIC RELATIONS FUNCTION

1.	LEARNING OBJECTIVES (OUTCOMES)	215
2.	INTRODUCTION	215
3.	DEFINITION OF THE FUNCTION	218
4.	OBJECTIVES OF PUBLIC RELATIONS	221
5.	INTEREST GROUPS	222
6.	SHAPING PUBLIC OPINION	225
7.	METHODS OF COMMUNICATION	229
8.	SOCIAL RESPONSIBILITY	230
9.	SUMMARY	232
10.	SELF-EVALUATION	232
11.	REFERENCES	234

PREFACE

A small business is not merely a small big business. Small enterprises have requirements and objectives that are quite distinct from those of large organisations. As the authors of this management textbook, we have been keenly aware of this distinction in giving you, the owner and manager of a small enterprise, the basic information that will help you to manage your business for optimum success.

The aim of this book is to teach you the principles of the eight enterprise functions that are essential for managing a small business successfully. These eight functions are: general management, finance, marketing, operations, purchasing, human resources, administration and public relations.

As a small business manager, you will have to be well informed about all these functions. The emphasis on the various functions may differ in different businesses; for example, one business might be market-oriented and another more operations-oriented. Nevertheless, a decision about marketing, for example, will inevitably have an influence on other functions like finance and operations. For this reason, every business will need to manage the eight functions, individually and collectively, in such a way that it achieves its main business objectives. In this book we will provide you with the basic guidelines on how to manage each function effectively without losing sight of its influence on the other functions.

The approach we have followed is practical, and you will be given specific pointers and advice on planning, developing and implementing the eight functions to increase the profitability of your enterprise and to enhance your potential to succeed.

The book has been written specifically for the South African market, with relevant case studies and examples of small businesses in an African context.

We wish you every success with your enterprise.

Cecile Nieuwenhuizen

KEY TO ICONS

Four icons are used throughout this text to depict different components of the interactive learning process:

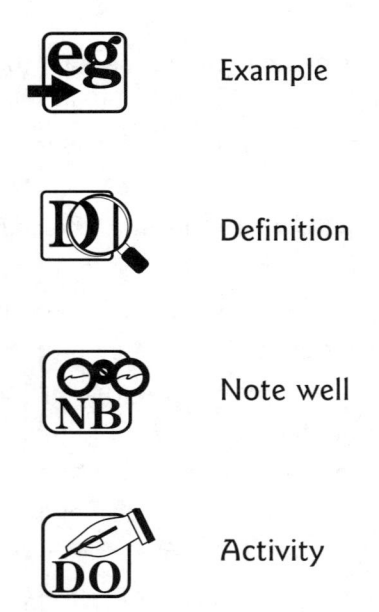

Example

Definition

Note well

Activity

1 GENERAL MANAGEMENT

1 LEARNING OBJECTIVES (OUTCOMES)

After you have studied this chapter, you should be able to:

- define planning;
- distinguish between long-, medium- and short-term planning;
- explain the steps in the planning process;
- analyse the organising function and explain how the organisation; structure serves as a framework for the activities of the enterprise;
- explain the steps in the organising process;
- define coordination as an additional management function;
- explain the importance of leadership in the enterprise;
- define and discuss control;
- explain the control process.

2 INTRODUCTION

In this chapter we will discuss general guidelines that can be used in the management of a small business. We often hear about small businesses going bankrupt. Unfortunately, poor management is very often the reason for these businesses not making the grade. Good management is therefore a prerequisite for a successful business.

Every business deals with various **organisation functions** or **enterprise functions**. The eight functions that occur in most businesses and that are discussed here are the following:

- The general management function;
- The financial function;
- The marketing function;

THE ENTREPRENEURSHIP SERIES

Management for Entrepreneurs

☞
- ❏ The operations function;
- ❏ The purchasing function;
- ❏ The human resources function;
- ❏ The administrative function;
- ❏ The public relations function.

In this chapter we will take a closer look at **general management**. Bear in mind, however, that there will always be interaction between this function and all the other functions.

What exactly do we mean by the concept of management? And how do we distinguish between good and bad management in a small business?

In the discussion that follows, we will try to answer these questions. Because management is such a broad concept, we will concentrate specifically on those aspects that apply to small businesses.

Most experts in the field of management divide the management function into **four main functions** and **six additional functions**, which are:

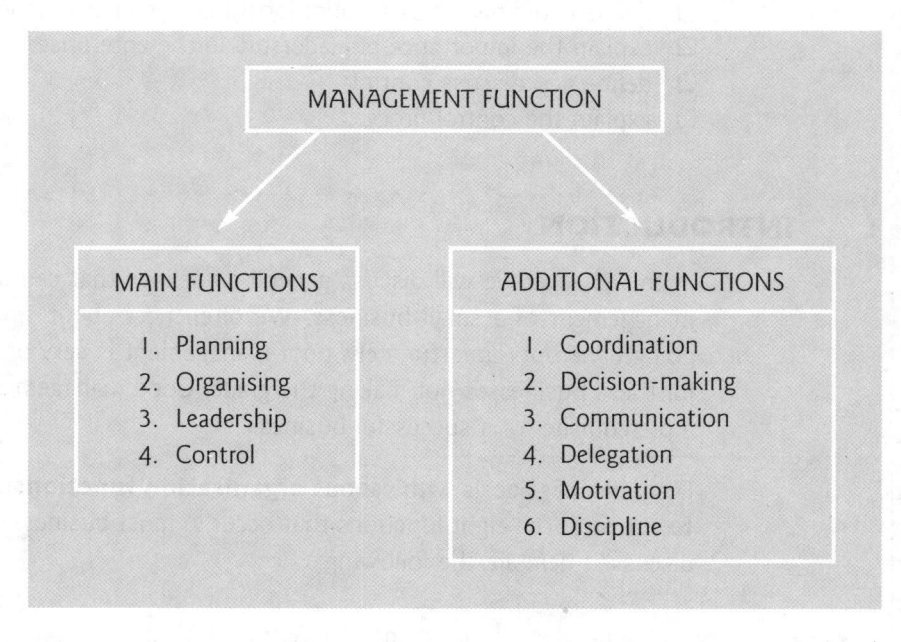

```
              MANAGEMENT FUNCTION
              /                \
    MAIN FUNCTIONS          ADDITIONAL FUNCTIONS
    1. Planning             1. Coordination
    2. Organising           2. Decision-making
    3. Leadership           3. Communication
    4. Control             4. Delegation
                           5. Motivation
                           6. Discipline
```

The basis of our discussion, and of the management process, is planning. After that we will look at organising, leading and control, and then at the six additional functions that apply directly to a small business.

CHAPTER 1
General Management

> **NB**
> We will discuss all these functions as separate aspects. In practice, however, they usually all combine to form **one activity**. In many cases it is difficult to distinguish these various functions from one another. You should therefore not regard the functions as separate from one another, but as parts, each of which is closely connected to the others to form a unit.

3 THE MAIN MANAGEMENT FUNCTIONS

Starting your own business is like building a house. Before you can start building, you must first lay the foundations. The management functions are the foundations on which you build your business. Planning, as the starting point of management, refers to the way in which you will lay the foundations for your business. Let us take a closer look at the factors that play a role in planning.

3.1 Planning

Planning is that aspect of management in which you determine in advance **what** you want to achieve with your business, and **how** you want to achieve it. When you plan, you draw up **objectives** for your business, and work out a **systematic plan** for achieving those objectives.

Planning is of vital importance to entrepreneurs. Remember, however, that you can make the best of plans, but if you do not carry out those plans, nothing will have been achieved.

> **eg**
> Assume you plan to start your own shoe shop. After considering all the aspects, you plan to do the following:
>
> | | |
> |---|---|
> | 3–5 April: | Develop your plans |
> | 6 April: | Find sales staff |
> | 7 April: | Make financial arrangements |
> | 9–13 April: | Search for suitable premises |
> | 16 April: | Obtain the necessary documentation and licence |
> | 17–18 April: | Place orders for provisional stock |

THE ENTREPRENEURSHIP SERIES

Management for Entrepreneurs

19–20 April: Order the necessary stationery and forms, and place advertisements in the media
23–24 April: Unpack and arrange stock
25 April: Open shop

You arrange that your stock will be imported from Italy by sea. However, the boat is delayed, and the stock arrives two weeks later than you planned. In addition, the exchange rate changes unexpectedly, and the shoes cost a lot more than you originally budgeted. Your shoe shop consequently cannot open on the target date.

From this example it is therefore very clear that you must both:

❑ **plan** the tasks carefully;
❑ **manage** the plan to ensure that all tasks are completed on time.

When you plan, your planning must be **realistic** and **flexible**. To ensure that your planning is realistic, you need **information**. This information is obtained largely from **past experience**. Information from past experience is important because it gives you perspective on the present to allow for realistic planning for the future.

Information from past experience is obtained from three environments, which are:

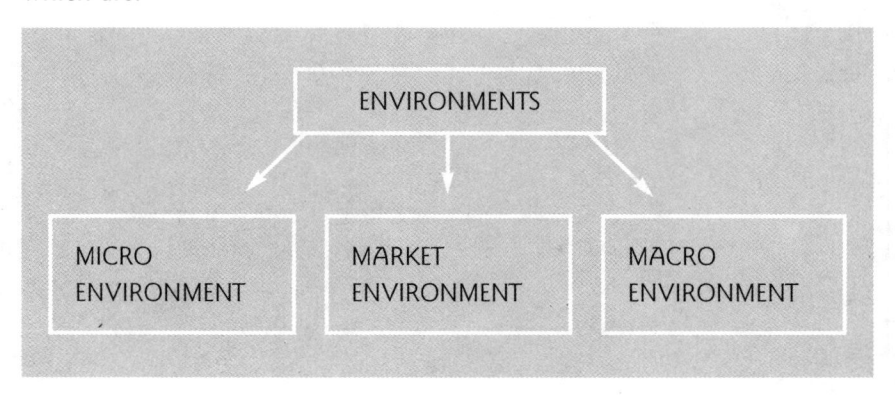

ENVIRONMENTS

MICRO ENVIRONMENT | MARKET ENVIRONMENT | MACRO ENVIRONMENT

CHAPTER 1
General Management

We will explain these briefly below.

The **micro environment** refers to aspects such as the enterprise's objectives, rules, regulations, policy, budget, decisions, plans and organisation structure.

The **market environment** refers to the interaction that takes place between your business and its immediate environment. The immediate environment includes the consumers and their needs, suppliers and creditors, staff and your competitors in the market.

The **macro environment** refers to the economic, political, social, technological and ecological factors in the environment. They are usually environmental forces that cannot affect your business directly.

1. Draw up your own summary of the section that you have just studied by filling in the missing words below.

```
                    ENVIRONMENTS
         ↙              ↓              ↘
```

MICRO-ENVIRONMENT (Business)	MARKET ENVIRONMENT	MACRO-ENVIRONMENT
❏ Objectives		❏ ....
❏ Rules and	❏ Consumers and their	❏ Political factors
❏	❏	❏ Social factors
❏	❏	❏ ....
❏	❏ .... in the market	❏ ....
❏		
❏ Organisation structure		

2. What should entrepreneurs do to ensure that their plans are realistic and flexible **and** that they are carried out?

....
....
....
....

THE ENTREPRENEURSHIP SERIES
Management for Entrepreneurs

Planning involves three aspects:
- long-term planning (or strategic planning);
- medium-term planning (or functional planning);
- short-term planning (or operational planning).

> **Long-term planning** involves the development of a broad, long-term strategy to reflect the mission of the business. The time-frame here stretches from three to ten years or longer. The planning is not done in specific detail, but **broad general guidelines** are drawn up to ensure that the business remains on track.
>
> **Medium-term planning** is derived from the long-term planning. It is aimed more **specifically** at the business's **activities**, and stretches over a term from one to three years. Here a plan is drawn up for every section of the business; for instance, for marketing, purchasing, finance and the operations section.
>
> **Short-term planning** usually stretches over not more than a year. It involves the **daily carrying-out of instructions** and the giving of instructions to certain people according to the set objectives.

During your planning, you will have to decide on the **main objective** and the **secondary objectives** of your business, and also what **resources** you will use. The main objective is the overall objective, which determines the direction of your business in the long term. The main objective of all small businesses is usually to make a profit. The secondary objectives are the additional objectives that you must set to achieve your primary objective. Resources are **all the things** that the business uses to achieve its objectives. They include natural resources such as land and buildings, human resources such as staff, and capital.

> Assume that you are the owner of a restaurant. In order to do short-, medium- and long-term planning, you will have to ask yourself questions such as the following:
>
> LONG-TERM PLANNING
> - What is my restaurant's primary objective? (For instance, to make a R3 500 profit per month.)

CHAPTER 1
General Management

- How can I best use my investments to ensure that the restaurant will still have capital over after ten years?
- Will I open a second restaurant on different premises within the next ten years?
- What human resources will I need to run the restaurant for the next ten years?
- Should I appoint an external consultant to take charge of the restaurant's advertising over the next five years?

MEDIUM-TERM PLANNING
- What are my restaurant's secondary objectives? (For instance, to have a minimum of 60% of capacity per day.)
- What is my budget for the next three years?
- Will the shopping centre in which my restaurant is situated still be as popular in three years' time as it is today?
- What training should I give my staff over the next three years to ensure that the service my restaurant offers is still excellent?
- How will I advertise my restaurant over the next year – in the media, or by printing pamphlets?

SHORT-TERM PLANNING
- What must I do to make my restaurant's opening day a success?
- How can I make as much profit as possible over the next six months?
- How many waiters should I appoint in the next few months?

7

THE ENTREPRENEURSHIP SERIES

Management for Entrepreneurs

❑ How should I go about ensuring the presence of a journalist or two on opening day?

Now think of your own business, or one that you intend to open. What aspects should you consider over the long term, medium term and short term?

LONG-TERM PLANNING

....
....
....
....
....
....
....

MEDIUM-TERM PLANNING

....
....
....
....
....
....
....

SHORT-TERM PLANNING

....
....
....
....
....
....
....

CHAPTER 1
General Management

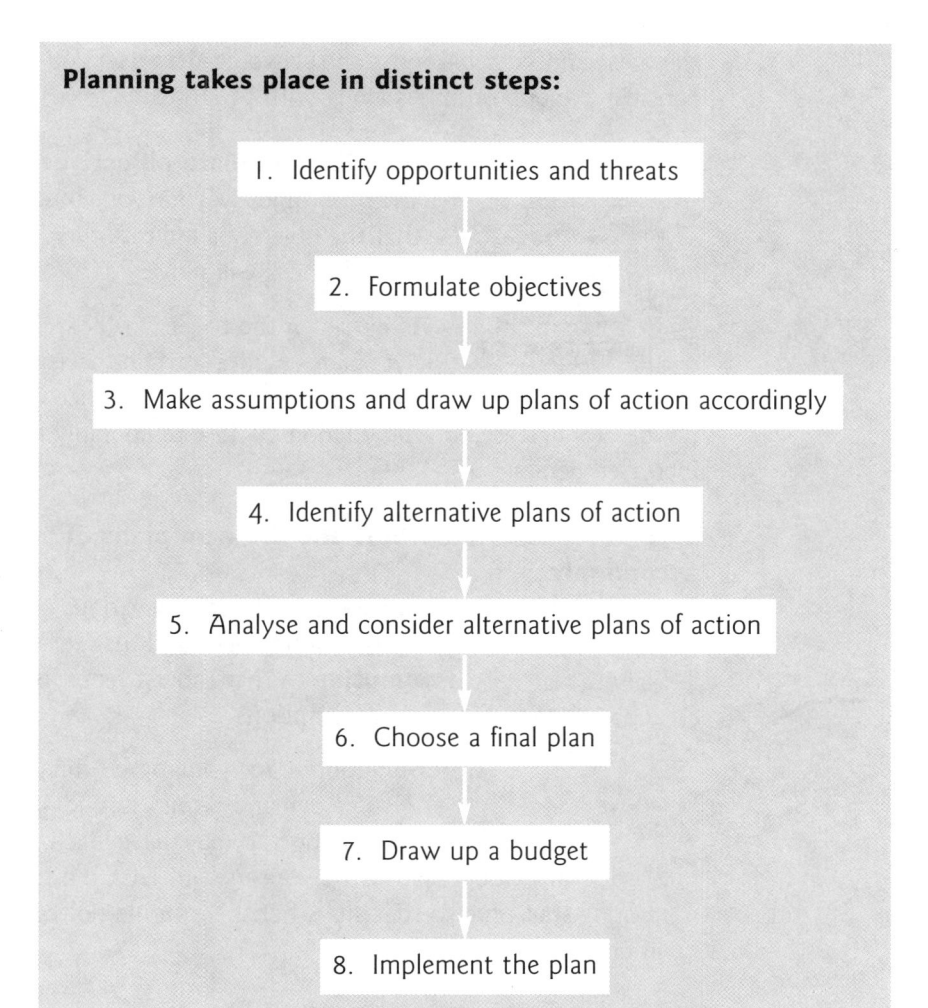

Planning takes place in distinct steps:

1. Identify opportunities and threats
2. Formulate objectives
3. Make assumptions and draw up plans of action accordingly
4. Identify alternative plans of action
5. Analyse and consider alternative plans of action
6. Choose a final plan
7. Draw up a budget
8. Implement the plan

Step 1: Identify opportunities and threats

Before you formulate any plans, you should consider all the various opportunities and threats that could affect your business. As the owner, you should have a clear picture of your business so that you can evaluate all these opportunities and threats. For instance, what are the chances that your market will increase or decrease?

Assume that you own a bakery in Mossel Bay. When Mossgas arrived, you foresaw that your market and turnover would increase. You therefore had an opportunity to expand. However, you should also have taken into account that the increase in your market would last only a short while. After the building of Mossgas, most workers would leave the area, and your bakery's market would decrease. You should therefore consider the opportunities along with the threats.

Step 2: Formulate objectives

Draw up objectives for your business. Remember that the objectives indicate the direction in which your business will move.

As owner of the bakery in Mossel Bay, you would have had to take certain decisions about your increased market. For instance, you may have decided to increase your production by 45% temporarily to provide for the increased demand.

Step 3: Make assumptions and draw up plans of action accordingly

Study the information you have gained from the various environments (the micro, market and macro environments) and use it to make certain **assumptions**. Then adjust your plans to each of those assumptions.

Assumption 1 for your bakery may have been that the greater demand would last for two years before decreasing. Assumption 2 may have been that the greater demand would last for three years, but that the town would grow during that time so that after that there would not be such a decrease in demand.

Step 4: Identify alternative plans of action

Now develop alternative plans to provide for all the assumptions that you have made.

In the case of Assumption 1, you may have planned to employ more temporary staff to provide for the increased demand. In the case of Assumption 2, you may have purchased more ovens to increase production capacity.

Step 5: Analyse and consider the alternative plans of action

Now weigh up the various plans against one another and look at the advantages and disadvantages of each plan. Make sure that you consider each plan from every angle and know exactly what effect each will have on your business.

CHAPTER 1
General Management

The advantage of the bakery's first plan (Assumption 1) is, for instance, that you will have to pay the salaries of temporary staff for a certain period only. One disadvantage is that the time that you devote to their training is not compensated for fully in their employment.

Step 6: Choose a final plan

Now decide which plan or plans you will follow.

For instance, you may decide that Assumption 1 is more realistic. You will therefore not purchase extra ovens to provide for increased demand, but will rather employ people to work in shifts.

Step 7: Draw up a budget

Before you can put your plans into operation, you must draw up a budget. This will ensure that you have the necessary financial resources to carry out those plans.

Does the bakery have sufficient funds to cover the salaries of temporary workers?

Drawing up the budget is one of the most important aspects of planning in any business. We will deal with budgeting in more detail in Chapter 2.

Step 8: Implement the plan

Now implement the plan you have decided on, and make provision for supporting plans.

For instance, the bakery will advertise for temporary staff, and will start training more bakers.

THE ENTREPRENEURSHIP SERIES
Management for Entrepreneurs

> **DO**
>
> What aspects will you have to bear in mind before you implement a final plan for your business?
>
> ....
> ....
> ....
> ....
> ....

3.2 Organising

Your business will not benefit from the objectives that are formulated and the plans that are compiled if there is no organisation in your business.

Organising takes place when two or more people work together to achieve a common purpose. This means that you must determine in advance **how, where, by whom, when** and **with what resources** the jobs must be carried out to achieve the objectives of the business. Such decisions will also give your business an **organisational structure**.

> **Organisation** as a management function deals mainly with the following:
> ❑ The grouping and allocation of activities to main sections and subsections;
> ❑ The creation of posts within those sections;
> ❑ Decisions on duties, authority and responsibilities.

Take the example of a garage. To start with, there are just four people: the owner and three petrol pump attendants. The organisation structure is illustrated in Figure 1.1.

Figure 1.1

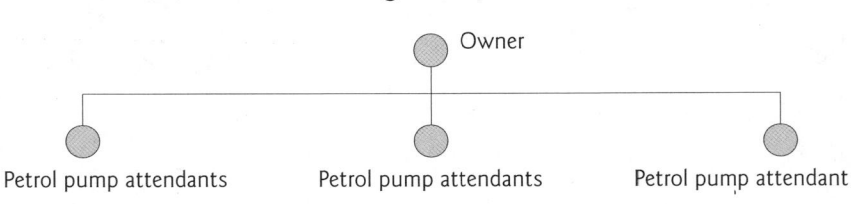

```
                    Owner
          ┌───────────┼───────────┐
          │           │           │
  Petrol pump    Petrol pump    Petrol pump
  attendants     attendants     attendant
```

CHAPTER 1
General Management

As the business grows, the owner appoints two mechanics, with a helper for each. The organisation structure is now as follows:

Figure 1.2

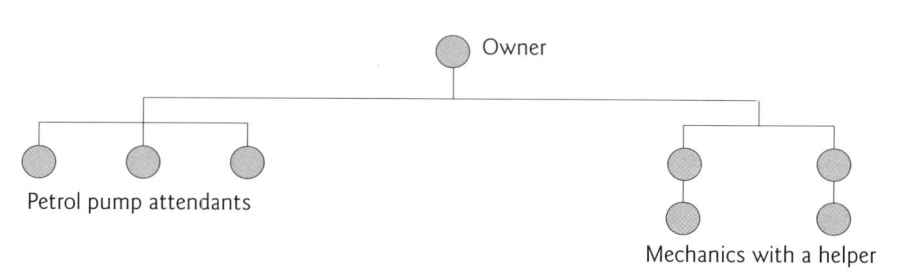

Owner
Petrol pump attendants
Mechanics with a helper

Still later, the owner opens a tuck shop. He appoints someone to work in the shop, and another two petrol pump attendants. The organisation structure is now illustrated in Figure 1.3.

Figure 1.3

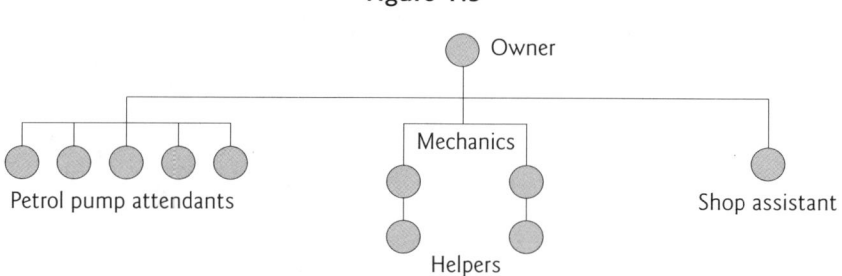

Owner
Petrol pump attendants
Mechanics
Helpers
Shop assistant

However, it is important to note that you will often have to use **skilled people from outside the business** to perform certain duties. As a small business owner, you will often not have sufficient funds to appoint people for all possible tasks, and this will also not be profitable. For instance, the owner of the garage will probably use an accountant on a **part-time basis**. Together with the petrol company, he may also appoint marketing agents on a **contract basis** to help with the marketing of the garage. These people also form part of the organisational structure, although they are not always employed full-time. The organisational structure will then be as follows:

THE ENTREPRENEURSHIP SERIES

Management for Entrepreneurs

Figure 1.4

```
                        Owner
           ┌──────────────┴──────────────┐
      FULL-TIME STAFF              PART-TIME STAFF
      ┌────┬────┴────┐              ┌──────┴──────┐
                                Accountant    Marketing
  Petrol pump   Mechanics      Shop            agents
  attendants    and helpers    assistant
```

Use this space to illustrate the organisation structure in your existing or proposed business.

To ensure that the organising function is as effective as possible, organising must be done **logically** and **systematically**. The best way of doing this is to follow a certain **procedure**, by which one step follows another. Assume that you are the owner of a car tyre business. We will now explain how you can use the following steps to advantage in your business:

CHAPTER 1
General Management

```
1. Gather the necessary information
            ↓
2. Identify and analyse activities
            ↓
3. Group related tasks together
            ↓
4. Divide the workload according to resources
            ↓
5. Allocate responsibilities and authority
            ↓
6. Obtain the necessary resources and announce arrangements
```

1. Gather the necessary information

As the owner of a car tyre business, you should gather information to help you achieve the objectives of the business, taking the budget into account. Once you have the information, decide on a **systematic way of working**. The working method must not conflict with the stated policies of the business. Also take available resources into account to ensure that you achieve your goals.

2. Identify and analyse activities

Now investigate and analyse all the possible activities, such as the replacement of tyres and exhaust systems, and the attachment of towbars. After this, decide which activities are important for your business to achieve its goals.

3. Group related tasks together

Divide the tasks that occur in the business as a whole into logical groups, such as workshop functions, financial functions, marketing functions and so forth. Then allocate each of the functional groups to a specific person or group of people. Every employee must then perform **only** his or her allocated tasks. This prevents duplication of work and makes the best use of staff and other resources. In the car tyre business, for instance, it is important for the same person always to be at the counter.

4. Divide the workload according to resources

You must determine exactly the size of the workload of each of the various groups in your business. Determine, for instance, how much work there will be for the workshop mechanics. This information will enable you to decide how many people you should appoint to your team of mechanics. If there are too few employees in a team, they will feel that they never manage to get through their work, and their motivation will consequently suffer. However, if there are too many employees in a certain team, your labour costs will be higher than you can afford.

5. Allocate responsibilities and authority

All employees must be precisely informed about:

- what their responsibilities are;
- to whom they should report;
- from whom they may receive instructions.

Assume a worker, William, is instructed to put four Firestone 155/12 tyres onto a car. While he removes the old tyres from the car, the client decides rather to have four Continental 155/12s. William must know that he may comply with the customer's request, but that it is now his responsibility to make the change on the job-card so that the cashier can calculate the correct prices on the tyres. In a business, this sort of interaction between employees is very important.

6. Obtain the necessary resources and announce arrangements

To implement the plans, everything that the business needs, such as natural and human resources, procedures and budgets, must be available at the right times and in the right places. The relevant staff must then be informed of the arrangements, so that the work can be started on time and carried out.

CHAPTER 1
General Management

The organising function therefore involves coordinating the tasks of individual employees in such a way that the **joint effort will be more productive** than the sum total of individual efforts. This is also known as **synergy**. Effective organisation in a business therefore leads to synergy.

1. Explain in your own words what is meant by **synergy**.

   ....
   ....
   ....

2. Why must employees know exactly what their responsibilities are, from whom they may receive instructions and to whom they must report?

   ....
   ....
   ....

3.3 Leadership

Leadership is an extremely important part of the management process, because it assures the entrepreneur that the work will start and be completed.

Leadership indicates the relationship between one person, the leader, and the other members of the working group. This relationship must be such that the members of the working group will work together voluntarily to achieve the objectives of the group.

Leadership is the activity that takes place to ensure that the plans drawn up for the business are actually carried out to achieve the objectives of the business. The success or failure of a business is dependent on the leadership found in the business. In practice there are many examples of struggling businesses that were converted into successful organisations through exemplary leadership. However, the opposite is also true: successful businesses have also failed as a result of poor leadership. A good example of the effects of leadership is a restaurant, where customers can often see clearly how a new manager has a positive or negative effect on the business.

A number of different **leadership styles** can be identified. **Autocratic leaders**, for instance, feel that they must take all the decisions themselves, while **democratic leaders** feel that employees must share in decision-making. A leader with a '**laissez faire**' approach draws up objectives and guidelines for staff, and they must then continue on their own without any further leadership. A **task-oriented leader** places greater emphasis on the successful completion of tasks than on the needs and requirements of employees, while an **employee-oriented leader** places the needs of workers first.

There are many theories on leadership styles, and we will briefly look at the views of Blake and Mouton. These two writers have developed a managerial grid, which is shown below.

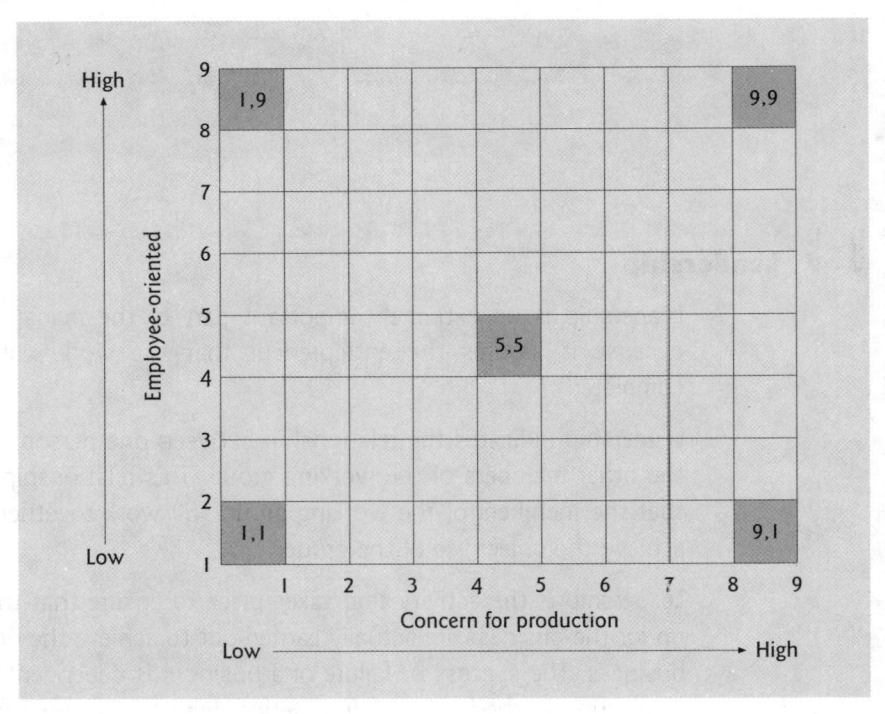

Figure 1.5

Source: Adapted from Blake & Mouton, 1964.

CHAPTER 1
General Management

	APPROACH	TYPE OF LEADER	LEADERSHIP STYLE
1.1	Little concern for employees or production	*Laissez faire* type	Poor leadership style
1.9	Little concern for production, but concerned about employees	Good Samaritan type	Employee-oriented style
9.1	Little concern for employees, but concerned about production	Autocrat	Task-oriented style
5.5	Reasonable interest in employees as well as in production	Compromise type	Maintains existing style of leadership
9.9	Greatest degree of concern for employees as well as for production	Democratic type	Team leadership style

Remember, however, that no leadership style will be perfect in all situations. A good leader must have the ability and the judgement to sum up the circumstances and to adapt his or her leadership style accordingly.

eg →

We can think here of the example of a nursery. Assume that you start a nursery with five workers and a cashier. At the start your leadership style will primarily be **task-oriented**, with little emphasis on the relationship between you and the workers. The reason for this is that the workers have no work experience yet; they must still receive instructions on their jobs and must become familiar with the rules and procedures of the nursery. If at this stage you do not give clear guidance, there will be chaos in the nursery.

19

THE ENTREPRENEURSHIP SERIES
Management for Entrepreneurs

However, as the workers become more familiar with their work, you may start to follow a more **employee-oriented approach**. When the workers have more experience and their skills increase, they will want to perform and will also be more willing to accept responsibility. You will then not need to exercise as much direct control over them.

Think again of the business you manage or hope to own. When would you follow (a) a task-oriented style and (b) an employee-oriented style?

(a) ....
....

(b) ....
....

3.4 Control

The above principles of good planning, organising and leading will be useless in the business if there is a lack of effective control. Control involves determining **realistic standards** by which employees' **actual performance** can be **measured**, so that any **deviations** in performance can be timeously traced. If deviations do occur, the necessary **corrective steps** can be taken so that the objectives set for the business are not jeopardised.

Good control therefore implies suitable **control systems** and **standards** to provide for the unique needs of the business. By motivating employees, you will be able to move away from direct supervision over them, to switch to a 'supervisory system' that includes not only control over employees, but also **quality assurance of products**.

The standards with which employees must comply must be determined carefully with the aid of information from the past, as well as information from related businesses in industry, to ensure that the objectives are realistic. The **employees must also accept the objectives** once you have explained what the standards are. The **performance of employees** can then be measured daily; in other words, measurement can take place

CHAPTER 1
General Management

continuously. If employees then do not achieve their daily objectives, you can investigate the reasons for this immediately, and corrective action can be taken as quickly as possible.

The control process consists of four steps:

1. Set standards, draw up methods for measuring performance, and announce the standards

2. Measure the actual performance

3. Evaluate and compare the actual performance with the standards

4. Take corrective action if necessary

To explain the steps better, we will use the example of a business that designs and makes clothes. The owner sells the clothes to five different boutiques. Two workers cut out patterns, and three other workers do the stitching.

1. Set standards, draw up methods for measuring performance, and announce the standards

Standards and criteria can be set for any task in the business. A criterion for the cutters, for instance, may be the number of patterns that they must cut out per day, and for the stitchers, the number of complete items they must stitch per day.

To ensure effective control, the standards must be set **realistically** and **clearly**. They must also be acceptable to the workers involved. The cutters, for instance, must be able quite easily to cut out ten patterns per day and must accept this as a reasonable standard.

THE ENTREPRENEURSHIP SERIES
Management for Entrepreneurs

2. Measure the actual performance

Remember that control is an ongoing process that must take place at the lowest possible cost. How often you measure performance will depend on what the relevant job entails. However, too long a period between the actual performance and the measurement would be fatal for the business. For instance, at the end of each day you should determine how many patterns the cutters have cut and how many items the stitchers have completed. Any **deviations** from the set standard must be traced as quickly as possible.

3. Evaluate and compare the actual performance with the standards

During this process, compare the performance of employees with the standards. In this way you will determine whether **deviations** have occurred and whether they will have a negative effect on the business. After this you can immediately take steps to correct the problem. For instance, if your production costs rise because of an increase in the cost of fabric, but the number of items of clothing that your workers make remains the same, you will have to do something to increase your profits.

4. Take corrective action if necessary

If performance does not comply with standards, steps will have to be taken to correct this. These steps may even bring about a change in the original standards. If a stitcher who could not meet the standards resigns, for instance, then it would be unfair to expect a new stitcher to complete in the first month the same number of items as an experienced stitcher. The standard will consequently have to be adjusted.

The control process described above will concentrate mainly on the areas of equipment, stock, staff, information and finance.

Answer the following questions briefly:

1. Why is it necessary to measure employees' performance?
   ....
   ....
   ....

CHAPTER 1
General Management

2. With what three requirements must performance standards comply?

   ....
   ....
   ....

3. Why is it necessary to compare employees' actual performance with a performance standard?

   ....
   ....
   ....

4 THE ADDITIONAL MANAGEMENT FUNCTIONS

Coordination is an extremely important function because it combines all the other functions in your business. Below we will discuss it more fully, and also look briefly at the other five management functions.

4.1 Coordination

Coordination is the process in which the various functions in the business are treated as a functional unit so that the objectives of your business can successfully be achieved. Among other things it includes balancing and distributing the tasks of staff so that the best possible cooperation is achieved.

> The eight functions of the enterprise are discussed in the introduction to this chapter. Try to remember what they are, and then turn back to check on them.

As an entrepreneur, you are responsible for coordinating all these functions, and where you do not have the necessary knowledge or sufficient funds to employ someone full-time on these jobs, you can employ contract staff (outside staff) to fulfil the various functions. However, you are still ultimately responsible for all the functions.

THE ENTREPRENEURSHIP SERIES
Management for Entrepreneurs

> **NB**
>
> As we explained earlier on in this chapter, the main functions of general management are planning, organising, leadership and control. You need to coordinate all these functions to ensure that the management of your business is successful.

To fulfil the **financial function**, you may have to appoint an accountant. However, you will have to discuss your plans with the accountant so that he or she can determine whether you have sufficient funds to achieve your objectives and can draw up a budget providing for your plans for the business.

You may also have to use a marketing agent to manage the **marketing function** for the business. However, as with the accountant, you will have to inform the marketing agent of all your plans and objectives. This will allow him or her to work out a suitable marketing plan for you.

You will probably be in charge of the **operations function** yourself. However, you will have to coordinate your operations in such a way that they coincide with your marketing plan.

The **purchasing function** is another function that you may take charge of yourself. Bear in mind, however, that purchasing will have to be coordinated with the accountant and the financial function.

You may also decide to organise the **human resources function** yourself. However, before you appoint any new employees, you will have to consult with your accountant to find out whether there are sufficient funds to pay the salaries of additional employees.

For the **administrative function** you may appoint a part-time person, possibly mornings only, to perform the various tasks. This person is important in any business, because he or she will store information or data for you, for instance by filing orders, purchases and invoices. The other functions will therefore have to coordinate with the administrative function when they need any of the stored information.

As regards **public relations**, you may also appoint an outside person. This could possibly be the same person as your marketing agent. This person will help to ensure that your business becomes known in the area.

The eight functions of the enterprise are dealt with more fully in the chapters that follow.

CHAPTER 1
General Management

4.2 Decision-making

During decision-making, various possible solutions are considered for problems, and the best solution is chosen.

4.3 Communication

Communication involves the transfer of messages between the business and its external environment and within the business itself.

4.4 Motivation

Motivation is the process in which the entrepreneur persuades his or her employees that they should voluntarily do their work as well as possible.

4.5 Delegation

Delegation is the allocation of power or responsibility to subordinate employees.

4.6 Discipline

Discipline shapes the behaviour of employees so that their conduct helps to ensure the successful operation of the business.

Answer the following questions briefly:

1. Why is good communication between the owner of a business and her/his employees beneficial?

   ....
   ....
   ....
   ....

2. Why is it necessary for you as the owner of the business to motivate employees?

   ....
   ....
   ....

3. Why should you as the owner sometimes delegate tasks?

   ....
   ....
   ....

5 SUMMARY

Because management involves integrating the various functions, you as the entrepreneur will have to know about all the functions that occur in your business to be able to manage effectively. In your daily planning, organising, leadership and control, you must be supported by management principles. These principles are designed to create a healthy climate in the business, in which resources are used effectively to achieve goals.

The four basic management functions of planning, organising, leadership and control and the six additional functions cannot be isolated from one another, and must be applied as an integrated whole. This will ensure that as an entrepreneur you achieve your goals in the business.

6 SELF-EVALUATION

You work as an electrician for a large government corporation. This corporation is transferred to a private company and in the process your service and that of many others is terminated. You decide to start your own electrical company in the suburb in which you live.

1. Discuss your planning of the management function fully.

   ....
   ....

CHAPTER 1
General Management

....
....
....

2. What will your plans be in the:

SHORT TERM	MEDIUM TERM	LONG TERM
....	....	....
....	....	....
....	....	....
....	....	....
....	....	....
....	....	....
....	....	....
....	....	....

3. Explain the steps you would apply in the planning process to ensure that your planning goes well.

   1. ....
   2. ....
   3. ....
   4. ....
   5. ....
   6. ....
   7. ....
   8. ....

4. How can you use the organisation structure as a framework for your activities?

   ....
   ....
   ....
   ....

THE ENTREPRENEURSHIP SERIES
Management for Entrepreneurs

5. Write down the steps in the organisation process that you would use in your business.

   1. ....
   2. ....
   3. ....
   4. ....
   5. ....
   6. ....

6. Describe coordination as an additional management function, and indicate how you should coordinate the various management functions of your business.

   ....
   ....
   ....
   ....
   ....
   ....

7. Explain the importance of leadership in a business.

   ....
   ....
   ....
   ....
   ....

8. Describe the nature of the control that you would apply in your business.

   ....
   ....
   ....
   ....
   ....

CHAPTER 1
General Management

9. Explain the control process that you plan to follow in your business.

   ....
   ....
   ....
   ....
   ....

10. What word from column B best fits the description in column A? Write down only the letter of the answer.

A	B
1. The process in which the conduct of employees is shaped so that they help to ensure the success of the business. Answer:	(a) Motivation
2. The process of considering various solutions to problems and then choosing the best solution. Answer:	(b) Communication
3. The allocation of responsibilities and authority to subordinates. Answer:	(c) Discipline
4. The transfer of messages between the owner and employees and between the environment and the business. Answer:	(d) Decision-making
5. The process of persuading employees voluntarily to work to the best of their ability. Answer:	(e) Delegation

7 REFERENCES

Blake, R.R. & Mouton, J.S. 1964. *The Management Grid*. Houston, Texas: Gulf.

Boone, L.E. & Kurtz, D.L. 1999. *Contemporary Business*. 9th edition. Chicago: Dryden.

Certo, S.C. 2000. *Modern Management: Quality, Ethics, and the Global Environment*. 8th edition. Boston: Allyn & Bacon.

Cronje, G.J. de J., Neuland, E.W., Hugo, W.M. & Van Reenen, M.J. (eds) 2000. *Inleiding tot die Bestuurswese*. 4th edition. Johannesburg: Southern.

Dubrin, A.J., Ireland, R.D. & Williams, J.C. 1989. *Management and Organization*. Cincinnati: South-Western.

Du Plessis, P.G. (ed.) 1992. *Toegepaste Bedryfsekonomie: 'n Inleidende Oorsig*. 3rd edition. Pretoria: Haum.

Griffin, R.W. 1996. *Management*. 6th edition. Boston: Houghton.

Mondy, R.W., Sharplin, A.E., Flippo, E.B. 1988. *Management Concepts and Practices*. 4th edition. Boston: Allyn & Bacon.

2 THE FINANCIAL FUNCTION

1 LEARNING OBJECTIVES (OUTCOMES)

After you have studied this chapter, you should be able to:

- define the financial function in the small business;
- define financial management in the small business;
- distinguish between and explain the basic financial concepts;
- discuss the objectives of financial management;
- discuss the tasks of financial management.

2 INTRODUCTION

Any person establishing a small business would naturally like to make a success of it. Entrepreneurs also try to achieve a satisfactory return on the capital they have invested in a business. However, owners of small businesses cannot simply assume their businesses will be successful. They will not achieve their basic objectives without hard work and knowledge of the principles of financial management. They need **guidelines** to make effective decisions and to carry out tasks. In other words, owners of small businesses must follow **basic financial management guidelines** in the management of their financial activities.

The purpose of this chapter is to give you basic guidelines according to which you can manage the financial function in your business. If you apply these guidelines effectively, you are sure to achieve your business goals as well as your personal objectives.

We also look in particular at important financial concepts. Knowledge of these concepts is a prerequisite for effective financial management.

FINANCIAL FUNCTION AND FINANCIAL MANAGEMENT

A wide variety of activities takes place in a small business. Some of these activities are related to the manufacture of the product, sale of the product and the people working in the business (staff issues). Other activities are related in some way or another to finance in the business – the **financial activities**. Financial activities are part of the **financial function**, one of the eight functions in the enterprise.

Financial activities that take place in the small business include the following:

❑ Determining the amount of capital required by the business (what are the capital needs of the business?);
❑ Decision-making on how provision will be made for the capital need (financing the capital need);
❑ Record-keeping of all financial transactions and their results;
❑ Drawing up financial statements;
❑ Analysis of financial statements (what is the financial position of the business?);
❑ Drafting budgets;
❑ Collection of debts;
❑ Payment of creditors;
❑ Determining the owner's remuneration;
❑ Dealing with tax (personal taxes, value-added tax, income tax);
❑ Insurance matters (life insurance, unemployment insurance and physical insurance against fire and theft, for example).

The question is: what does the financial function in the small business involve?

The financial function refers to the activities in the small business that relate to:

❑ determining the **capital need** of the business and the composition of the need;

CHAPTER 2
The Financial Function

- determining the **best possible ways** of providing for the capital need (financing the need);
- **record-keeping** of all transactions and **analysis** of accounting data.

The financial activities of the business have to be approached in a planned and orderly manner. If these activities are not controlled, it will be impossible to achieve the objectives of the business. **The financial activities must be managed in a meaningful and orderly way**. To do this, you must apply the principles of **financial management**.

Financial management is management (planning, organisation and control) of the business's financial activities. The activities are managed so that the business can generate an income in the long term and can reach its objectives.

Financial management in the small business therefore actually amounts to the owner(s) taking the following **decisions**:

- What and how many assets (fixed and current assets) must the business acquire – in other words, what is the extent of the capital need? This is therefore a decision on **investment**.
- From what sources, in what forms and at what cost must the assets be financed? This is a decision on **financing**.
- How must the net income after tax be divided among the owner(s) and the business? (The net income is the income retained by the business after deduction of all its operating costs.) These decisions deal with **distribution of income**.
- How and in what way must the financial transactions and their results be recorded? These are decisions on **record-keeping**.

Fill in the missing words:
(i) The financial function refers to activities relating to ………… for the capital need, financing of the need, the …………… of net income between the owner and the business and ……………… of the financial transactions and the …………… of data.

(ii) Financial management deals with ………………………………………
……………………………………………………………………………………

THE ENTREPRENEURSHIP SERIES
Management for Entrepreneurs

> (iii) The owner(s) of the small business must make decisions on ...., financing, ... and .... in such a way that they contribute to the achievement of ....

4 BASIC FINANCIAL CONCEPTS[1]

Your knowledge of the basic financial concepts will affect the success of your business. It will enable you to know exactly what is referred to when, for instance, the bank manager inquires about the liquidity of your business, or when the accountant refers to the income statement or the balance sheet.

The financial concepts that we would like to emphasise are:

- capital;
- capital need;
- money and capital markets;
- investment;
- financing;
- profitability;
- liquidity;
- solvency;
- income statement;
- balance sheet.

Capital

Capital is the money available to the business for the purchase of goods and services with a view to generating an income for the business.

The business earns this income by buying and selling goods and services. Capital is therefore the value of the total assets of the business, expressed in monetary terms.

---

[1] The basic financial concepts are based on Chapter 1 in: Kritzinger, A.A.C. & Fourie, J.C.W. 1996. *Basic Principles of Financial Management for a Small Business.* Cape Town: Juta. Permission has been obtained from the publisher.

CHAPTER 2
The Financial Function

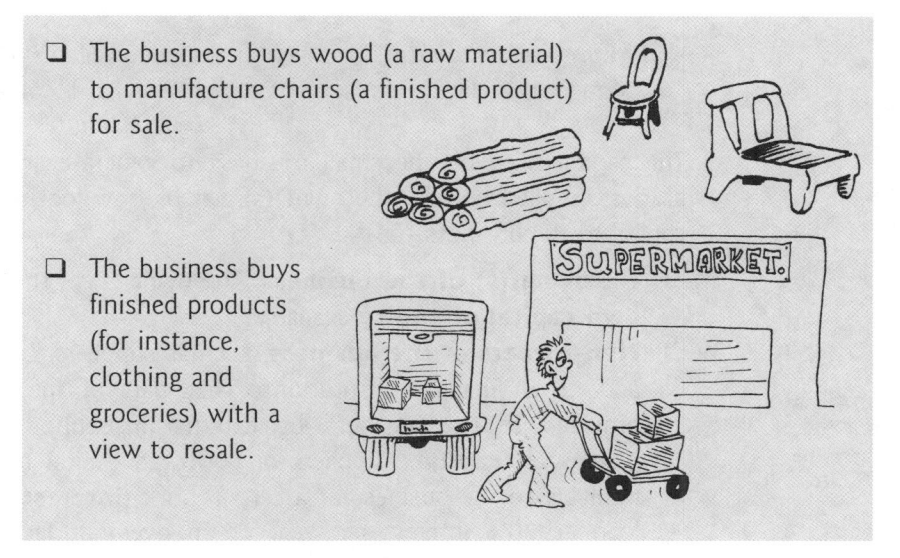

- The business buys wood (a raw material) to manufacture chairs (a finished product) for sale.

- The business buys finished products (for instance, clothing and groceries) with a view to resale.

The business uses the capital available to it to obtain goods (and services). Put in another way, the capital is used to obtain **assets**. We make a distinction between **fixed assets** and **current assets**.

- **Fixed assets** are items such as land, buildings, machinery and equipment. Fixed assets have a relatively long life and the business can therefore use them for longer periods. The capital used to obtain fixed assets is known as **fixed capital**.
- The business also uses part of its money for **current assets**, such as when it purchases stock or finances debtors. Current assets are items that can be converted into cash quickly or that are already in cash. The business requires current assets to be able to use its fixed assets (without raw material and stock, the machinery and equipment cannot be used). The capital used to obtain current assets is known as **operating or working capital**.

Capital is made available to the small business over **various periods**. It may be available over the **long, medium and short term**.

- **Short-term capital**. This capital is usually available for a period of between one and three years. However, in most cases the period is one year or less.
- **Medium-term capital**. Capital over the medium term is usually available for a period of between one and five years.

THE ENTREPRENEURSHIP SERIES

Management for Entrepreneurs

> ❑ **Long-term capital**. This capital is made available for a period of longer than five years, such as a period of 10, 15 or 20 years.

The capital used by the small business to generate an income is not always supplied only by the owner(s). Let us now look at who provides capital to the business:

❑ The **owner(s) of the business**. The owner(s) of the business make **own capital or equity** available.

❑ **Non-owners of the business**, such as suppliers, commercial banks and other financial institutions. That part of the capital lent or provided to the business by external institutions is known as **borrowed capital**. Suppliers of borrowed capital make the capital available to the business at a certain price (**interest**), for instance a loan at 20% interest per year or an overdraft facility at a bank. Normally interest must be paid on borrowed capital, but in certain cases it is possible to obtain capital without having to pay interest on it. Credit from suppliers (supplier credit or trade credit) is also a form of borrowed capital. Suppliers grant this when a business buys stock or raw materials on credit from them. Normally no interest is charged on such credit. Interest is only charged in cases in which the account is not paid within the agreed period.

What word from column B fits best with the description in column A? Write down only the letter of the answer.

A	B
Used to purchase stock Answer:	(a) Borrowed capital
Capital made available by the owner(s) of the business Answer:	(b) Working capital
Capital available for less than one year Answer:	(c) Medium-term capital

CHAPTER 2
The Financial Function

Capital available for between one and five years Answer:	(d) Own capital
Capital made available by financial institutions and suppliers Answer:	(e) Short-term capital

Capital need

> The **capital need** of a small business is the need for money to obtain goods and services with which the business can set about generating an income.

We distinguish between the **permanent capital need** and the **variable capital need**. This distinction is made on the following basis:

❑ **Permanent capital need**: This is that part of the capital need that the business constantly needs in order to function profitably. The permanent capital need consists of the need for fixed assets on the one hand and current assets on the other.
❑ **Variable capital need**: The business sometimes needs more capital and sometimes less. The variable capital need is that part of the capital need that the business only needs from time to time.

A furniture manufacturer always needs machinery and equipment (fixed assets), wood, glue and varnish (current assets) to be able to function effectively. A restaurant must also always be able to buy fresh meat and vegetables or it will not be able to serve meals. This continuous need for fixed assets and current assets is the permanent capital need.

THE ENTREPRENEURSHIP SERIES
Management for Entrepreneurs

> The owner of a toyshop usually experiences an increased demand for toys during December. Parents like to buy toys as gifts and the owner must then have sufficient stocks. The increased stock levels result in a greater capital need. This additional capital need is what is known as the variable capital need.

Money and capital markets

The small business may obtain capital from sources in either the money market or the capital market.

- The **money market** makes capital available in the **short term** – these are periods of less than one to three years. Examples are a short-term loan over 12 months, or a bank overdraft facility at any commercial bank.
- The **capital market** makes funds available over the **medium and long term** – that is, for periods longer than three years. An example is a 20-year mortgage bond on a building through a commercial bank.

Investment

You now know that the business uses capital to buy fixed assets (such as land and buildings) and current assets (such as stock) with the purpose of generating an income. The business **invests** the capital in assets.

Financing

The business must make the necessary funds available to obtain assets. We call this process the **financing** of the capital need. Financing, in other words, involves making **provision for the business's capital need**. The capital is made available to the business by the owners and/or external financial institutions (capital suppliers).

CHAPTER 2
The Financial Function

Do you agree with the following statements? Tick your answer in the relevant column.

	YES	NO
❏ The business invests capital in fixed assets as well as in current assets	....	....
❏ The capital need of a business is always financed with equity (own capital)	....	....
❏ Capital is available from the capital market in the short term	....	....
❏ A loan over six months is made available by the money market	....	....

Profitability

The business obtains assets with the exclusive purpose of generating an income (making a profit). The owner/s of the business want to earn a certain **profitability** on the capital.

Profitability refers to the relationship between the net income earned over a certain period, and the capital used in that period to generate the income. Profitability is expressed as a percentage.

Profitability is calculated as follows:

$$\frac{\text{net income earned}}{\text{total capital}} \times 100\%$$

The net income earned by a business during the past year is R20 000. The capital used during the year to earn that income was R100 000. The profitability of the capital is:

$$\frac{20\ 000}{100\ 000} \times 100\%$$
$$= 20\%$$

Profitability is discussed in more detail in section 5.

Liquidity

The business will incur certain expenditure and make certain payments in the process of making an income. Examples of payments the business must make are payments to suppliers, interest payments, wages and salaries, rental, water and electricity. **Liquidity** refers to the business's ability to keep making all these payments regularly and on time. We say that the business must be **liquid**.

Solvency

The ability of the business to pay off its debt at any time – even should its activities stop – is known as the **solvency** of the business. Total assets must cover total liabilities of the business (liabilities are what the business owes to its creditors and suppliers of capital). This means, in fact, that the business's total assets must at least equal or exceed its total liabilities. When the business's total liabilities exceed its total assets, the business is technically insolvent.

Income statement

The income statement gives a **summary** of the business's **income and expenditure** over a certain period. The income statement is drawn up for a particular financial period (for instance, from 1 January 20xx to 31 December 20xx). The net income (or loss) for that particular period is clear from the income statement.

Balance sheet

The balance sheet gives an indication of the **financial position** of the business **at a certain point in time**. The balance sheet is drawn up at the end of the financial period; for instance, 31 December 20xx.

Explain the following financial concepts briefly. Write down only keywords – long sentences are unnecessary.

❑ Permanent capital need ....
   ....
❑ Money and capital markets ....
   ....
❑ Investment ....
   ....

CHAPTER 2
The Financial Function

❏ Liquidity...
....

❏ Solvency...
....

❏ Income statement ....
....

5 OBJECTIVES OF FINANCIAL MANAGEMENT

What is the purpose of financial management?

I want my capital to work to earn an income and make a profit

The **primary objective** of the small business is to gain maximum return on the capital invested in the business. Simply put, the business wants to make a **profit**. The owner(s) of the small business would like the business to be profitable, to grow and to succeed. Without a satisfactory return, this will not happen. The owners could otherwise have invested the capital that they put into the business at a bank and earned interest on it.

The primary objective of financial management is exactly the same as that of the business: **maximum return on capital over the long term**. **Maximising profitability** is therefore the primary objective of the small business and of financial management. The owners try to achieve the highest possible profitability on the capital that is available. This means that the owners try to earn the highest possible net income with the capital available to them.

THE ENTREPRENEURSHIP SERIES
Management for Entrepreneurs

> Do you still remember how to calculate profitability? Turn back to section 4 if you are uncertain.

> We can now make a distinction between **enterprise profitability** (the profitability of the enterprise) and **profitability of own capital**.
>
> ❑ **Business profitability** is the profitability earned during a specific period on **total capital (borrowed capital plus own capital) invested** in the business.
> ❑ **Profitability of own capital** refers to the profitability earned on **capital invested by the owners in the business**. (To calculate profitability of own capital, you therefore exclude total borrowed capital in the business.) Income earned with own capital is the net income that remains after all interest payments have been made. Profitability of own capital is determined by expressing this income as a percentage of own capital.

> The owner of a coffee shop opened the shop on 1 March with R50 000 capital. She made R25 000 of her own capital available and borrowed the rest (R25 000) from the bank at 15% interest a year. She used part of the money to buy tables, chairs, tablecloths and crockery. The rest of the money she used to buy stock and to finance operating costs (such as rental, wages and telephone) for the first few months.
>
> A year later, on 29 February, the books showed that the business returned a net income of R10 000 for the preceding 12 months before interest payments. The business paid R3 750 in interest over this period.

CHAPTER 2
The Financial Function

The business profitability for this period was 20%. This is calculated as follows:

$$\text{Profitability (business)} = \frac{\text{net income before interest paid}}{\text{total capital invested}} \times 100\%$$

$$= \frac{10\,000}{50\,000} \times \frac{100\%}{1}$$

$$= 20\%$$

Profitability of own capital for the period was 25%. This is calculated as follows:

$$\text{Profitability (own capital)} = \frac{\text{net income after interest}}{\text{own capital invested}} \times 100\%$$

$$[R10\,000 - R3\,750] = \frac{6\,250}{25\,000} \times \frac{100\%}{1}$$

$$= 25\%$$

At the end of 2001 a car dealer earned a net income of R150 000 before interest. The total capital invested to earn this income was R800 000. The dealer supplied 40% of the total capital himself, while a financial institution made the rest available to the business at 18% interest per year.

Underline the correct answers:

❑ Profitability of the enterprise was (18%; 18,75%; 19,88%)
❑ Profitability of own capital was (18%; 18,75%; 19,88%)

Besides the **primary objective** of financial management, there are also **secondary objectives**. These objectives contribute in the end to the primary objective of maximising profitability.

THE ENTREPRENEURSHIP SERIES
Management for Entrepreneurs

Figure 2.1

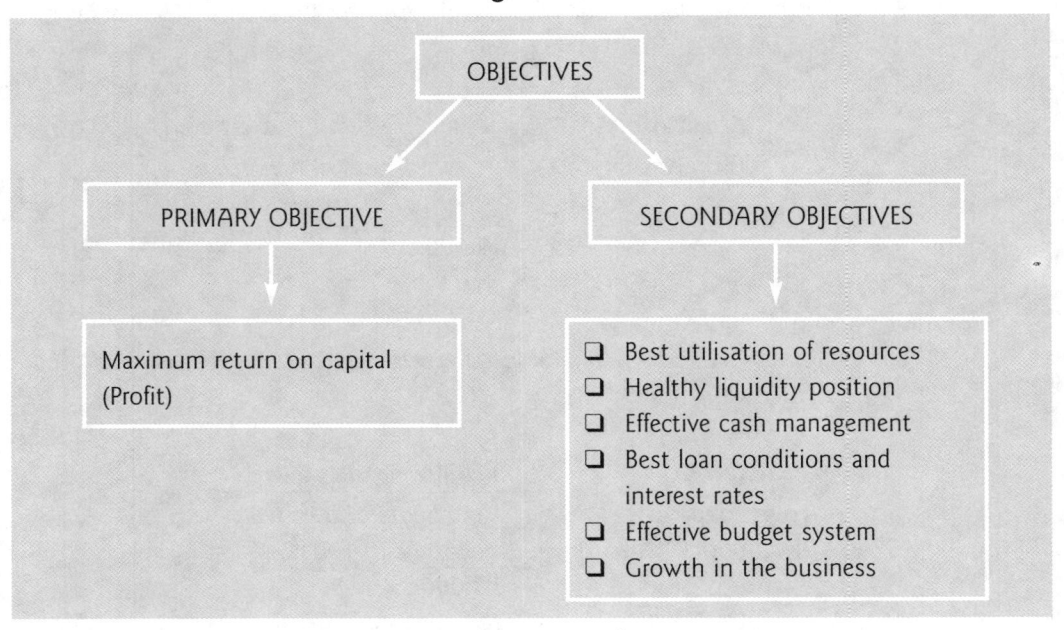

```
                    OBJECTIVES
                   /          \
       PRIMARY OBJECTIVE      SECONDARY OBJECTIVES
```

Primary Objective:
Maximum return on capital (Profit)

Secondary Objectives:
- Best utilisation of resources
- Healthy liquidity position
- Effective cash management
- Best loan conditions and interest rates
- Effective budget system
- Growth in the business

The following are secondary objectives of financial management:

Use scarce resources as well as possible
In this case the resource is specifically **capital**. The small business often has a shortage of sufficient capital, or the owners have certain limitations that prevent them from getting sufficient capital. The capital they do have is therefore a valuable resource and should be used as effectively and profitably as possible.

A laundry is positioned near a large townhouse complex. Many of the inhabitants make use of this facility.

The laundry has six large commercial washing machines and three tumble-driers. The owner is considering putting in another two washing machines to provide for customer needs (customers

CHAPTER 2
The Financial Function

must normally wait at least 20 minutes before a washing machine is available). He is also considering putting in another tumble-drier. However, many people use the washing machines and not the tumble-driers.

The owner has limited capital that he wishes to use as profitably as possible. Although the business also needs a tumble-drier, the owner buys only two washing machines. His capital is limited and it is more profitable for him to buy the washing machines because more people use them.

Maintain a healthy position of liquidity

Do you still remember what liquidity is? Refresh your memory by writing down keywords below.

....
....
....
....

For small businesses, a healthy position of liquidity can mean the difference between **growth and success** on the one hand, or failure on the other. Many small businesses that provide good products at competitive prices in active markets have nonetheless failed as a result of problems with liquidity. The business lands in a situation in which compulsory payments (payments to creditors, rental, water and electricity) can no longer be made in the short term. If this is the case, and the problems cannot be overcome, the business will fail.

You can achieve a healthy liquidity position by ensuring an effective **working capital cycle** in your business. This means that the business must as quickly as possible try to free capital tied up in working capital such as stock and debtors. This will allow the business to use this capital again for other needs.

THE ENTREPRENEURSHIP SERIES
Management for Entrepreneurs

eg

Pen & Pencil is a stationery shop that also sells to customers on credit.

Working capital is invested in cash, stock and debtors.

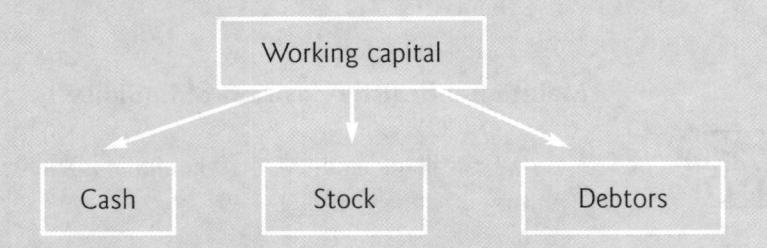

```
           Working capital
          /       |       \
       Cash     Stock    Debtors
```

The working capital cycle at Pen & Pencil is therefore as follows:

- Pen & Pencil buys stationery for cash and on credit. This means that the cash levels of the business drop and creditors increase.
- Pen & Pencil sells stationery for cash and on credit. This leads to an increase in the cash levels as well as an increase in debtors.
- Pen & Pencil pays its creditors and short-term obligations – the cash levels of the business drop.
- Pen & Pencil's debtors pay their accounts and the cash levels of the business rise.

```
    Cash ←─┐
           │
    Stock ─┤
           │
    Debtors│
           │
    Creditors ─┘
```

CHAPTER 2
The Financial Function

Apply effective cash management
This secondary objective of financial management is directly related to the liquidity position of the business. A shortage of cash in the small business can seriously affect the activities of the business. If the business lands in a situation where it cannot pay the necessary accounts on time, the business will have cash-flow problems.

> **A positive cash flow can be ensured by the following:**
>
> ❑ Collect debtors as soon as possible.
> ❑ Eliminate unnecessary stock and ensure that the business does not overstock (keeping too much stock costs money).
> ❑ Eliminate products that are not profitable (do not keep capital unnecessarily tied up in such stock).
> ❑ Lease fixed assets, such as buildings, delivery vehicles and computer equipment, instead of buying them.
> ❑ Use the discounts offered by suppliers, such as bulk discounts.
> ❑ Keep operating costs as low as possible.
> ❑ Draw up a cash budget on a monthly basis – this enables the business to make suitable provision for possible shortages of cash and also to know when cash will be available.

Negotiate the best loan conditions and interest rates from financial institutions
Owners of small businesses must not simply assume that they cannot negotiate the best interest rates from their commercial banks. Lower interest rates mean **lower costs of capital**, and this in turn has a positive effect on the profit of the business. However, it is important to remember that the business must be in a position to make interest payments on borrowed capital regularly and in time. The business must be able to keep to the conditions of the loan.

Implement an effective budgeting system
Without the necessary financial planning and control, the business will not be able to achieve its objectives. Indeed, it is very difficult to achieve any objectives without planning – you will achieve objectives only if you know exactly what you are aiming at. An effective budgeting system in which you make provision for future activities is a useful aid to determining how much capital you need and how you should use the capital.

THE ENTREPRENEURSHIP SERIES

Management for Entrepreneurs

Budgets as part of the tasks of financial management are discussed in more detail in section 6.

Manage growth in the small business

Growth in the small business brings with it a greater need for capital – the business must purchase **more assets** and requires **more working capital** to be able to function. If the growth of the business is not managed (the business may grow too fast), this can even lead to the downfall of the business. If the business does not have enough capital to finance the growth, or cannot gain access to external sources of capital (such as a bank) to obtain additional capital, it is not ready to grow. A shortage of sufficient cash can also limit the growth of the business.

Growth in the small business should be managed as follows:

- ❏ Consider the additional need for capital.
- ❏ Investigate the business's access to sources of capital (does the business have sufficient access?).
- ❏ Monitor the current ratio of the business (the business's liquidity must remain favourable).

1. Explain the following objectives of financial management in two sentences each:

    ❏ Best utilisation of resources: ....
    ....

    ❏ Maintaining liquidity: ....
    ....

    ❏ Management of growth in the business: ....
    ....

2. What are the other objectives of financial management in your business? Explain each in a sentence. ....
    ....
    ....
    ....

CHAPTER 2

The Financial Function

6 TASKS OF FINANCIAL MANAGEMENT

The tasks of financial management, or the tasks performed by the owner or person responsible for financial management in the small business, are aimed at achieving the primary objective of the business.

> Briefly sum up the primary objective of your small business: ....
> ....
> ....

The tasks to be undertaken to achieve the objective of profitability in the business arise directly from the business's financial activities.

We will look at the following tasks:

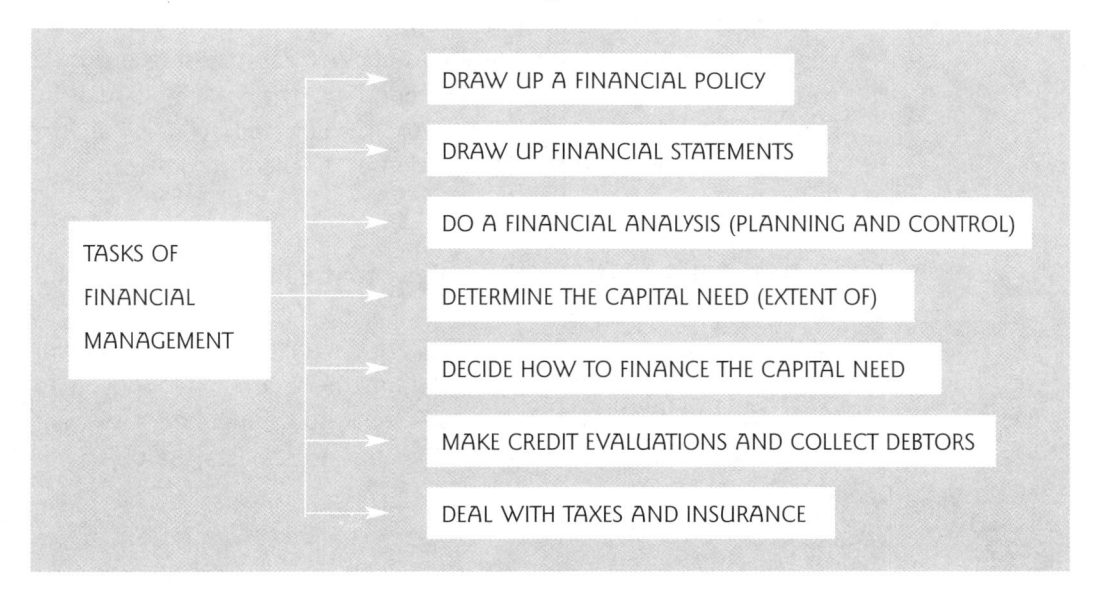

TASKS OF FINANCIAL MANAGEMENT
- DRAW UP A FINANCIAL POLICY
- DRAW UP FINANCIAL STATEMENTS
- DO A FINANCIAL ANALYSIS (PLANNING AND CONTROL)
- DETERMINE THE CAPITAL NEED (EXTENT OF)
- DECIDE HOW TO FINANCE THE CAPITAL NEED
- MAKE CREDIT EVALUATIONS AND COLLECT DEBTORS
- DEAL WITH TAXES AND INSURANCE

Draw up a financial policy
- ❏ **Formulate guidelines** according to which you will conduct your financial activities. This will help you to make logical decisions. For instance, determine the guidelines according to which you will grant credit, determine product prices, value stock and calculate the depreciation on assets.
- ❏ **Keep to the guidelines** formulated – this will ensure that your financial management is effective and that you achieve the business objective.

THE ENTREPRENEURSHIP SERIES

Management for Entrepreneurs

> A small business evaluates its stock to determine how much stock the business has and what its value is (in rands and cents). This information is necessary, among other things, when the financial statements are drawn up at the end of the financial bookyear.
>
> The business must decide according to which guidelines it will evaluate stock. For instance, will it use the last-in-first-out method, or the first-in-first-out method? (These concepts are explained in Chapter 4.)

Draw up financial statements
- It is important to have a **record-keeping system** that provides for the needs of your business. Financial statements are drawn up at the end of the financial period.
- If you cannot or do not want to keep the books yourself, appoint an **accountant or book-keeper** to do it for you. It will not always be necessary to appoint the person full-time; you can use someone on a part-time basis. However, it is important that there should be someone to take charge of the record-keeping and to draw up the financial statements. (More information on financial record-keeping is given in Chapter 7.)

Do a financial analysis with a view to financial planning and control
- With a financial analysis you investigate the financial position of your business. The information you get from the analysis allows you to apply **financial control**. This means that you can determine to what extent the actual performance of your business meets the objectives you have set for it.

> At the beginning of the year the owners of a small business aim to achieve at least a 20% return on the capital invested in the business. **The objective is therefore 20% profitability for the year.**
>
> At the end of the year the actual profitability achieved can be calculated from the financial statements. This can then be compared with the objective to see whether the 20% objective has been achieved or not. Assume that profitability of the business is only 12%. The owners must now investigate possible reasons for the poor performance.

CHAPTER 2
The Financial Function

> (These could be low sales and high operating costs.) In the period that follows, the business must try to eliminate the causes of the poor profitability figure by taking corrective steps, such as by wider marketing of the business's products.

Based on information obtained from the financial analysis, the business can **plan for a future period**. In the example above, the business has planned to eliminate the factors that have prevented it from achieving the objective of 20%. By basing financial planning on what happened in the past, the business has the opportunity to reduce and even eliminate the errors in the future.

Without financial planning it is impossible to achieve any effective objectives. (If they are achieved without planning, this is sheer luck!) **Financial planning means that the small business draws up plans and identifies actions to be carried out so that the objectives of the business can be achieved.**

A useful aid in financial planning is **budgets**. What is a budget?

> A **budget** is a plan, expressed in money, of all activities for a future period. It is therefore a money plan for a future period.

With the aid of a budget, the business determines expected income and expenditure for a future period. This information will then enable the business to determine how much capital it needs to be able to function effectively.

Determine the capital need
Capital need is affected by expected demand. A business that expects to sell 10 000 products has a greater capital need than one that expects to sell only 1 000 of the same products.

It is therefore essential that the business makes a **forecast of expected demand**. The best time to make the forecast is before you start drawing up the budgets for the period to come. Only when the business has information on expected sales can it start to draw up the sales budget. The other budgets follow the sales budget. **A forecast of expected demand is therefore the point of departure for drawing up the business's budgets.** What exactly is a sales forecast?

THE ENTREPRENEURSHIP SERIES
Management for Entrepreneurs

> A **sales forecast** is the estimate of expected sales for a future period – an approximate calculation of how many products the business expects to sell.

Now decide **how many and what assets** the business must obtain. Besides the capital required to purchase fixed assets (such as machinery, equipment and delivery vans), the business also requires capital to finance current assets. The business needs supplies (stock). If the business sells on credit, it needs capital to finance the debtors. In addition, it always needs cash to pay for its daily activities (such as wages, rental, water and electricity, insurance, the accountant, fuel and so on).

Decide how to finance the capital need

Decide from what sources the capital need will be financed. Financing is available from **internal and external sources**. Internal sources are available in the business itself, such as own capital and reserves, or profit put back into the business. External sources are sources outside the business that make capital available to the business. Examples are financial institutions (commercial banks, development corporations) and suppliers who sell to the business on credit.

Figure 2.2

```
                        SOURCES
                       /        \
          INTERNAL SOURCES      EXTERNAL SOURCES
                 |                      |
         The business itself     Financial institutions and
         ❑ Own capital           suppliers
         ❑ Reserves              ❑ Loans
                                 ❑ Trade credit
```

Remember, it is very difficult to attract capital from external sources if the owner(s) of the business do not also make a contribution. External capital suppliers want to know what the owner's level of commitment to his or her business is; they are usually not prepared to carry alone the risk that the business might fail.

Decide **when and for how long** you need the capital. Do you need short- or long-term capital? It is important that the type of financing is right for the type of need. For instance, it is highly unlikely that you would buy a building with a bank overdraft facility – you would rather use a long-term loan. Your bank manager can also give you valuable advice on how to adapt your type of financing to your needs.

Always maintain a **good relationship** with your bank, because this will in many cases be the place that helps you when you need financing.

Make credit evaluations and collect debts
If your business sells on credit, you must judge the **creditworthiness** of each customer and decide whether it will be worthwhile granting credit to this person. If the risk of non-payment is too high, it will not be worth selling on credit. Credit sales must have a positive effect on the profit of the business. If this is not the case, you should reconsider your decision to grant credit.

You must also decide **on what terms** the business will grant credit. Decide, for instance, how long the credit period should be (for instance, 30 days), whether you will grant cash discounts if the debtor pays before a certain date, and whether you will charge interest on overdue accounts.

Credit sales mean **additional administration**, such as accounts that must be written up and sent out, and overdue debts that must be collected.

Ensure that accounts are **correct** and are sent out **on time**. If not, your accounts will be paid late. Late accounts must be collected as soon as possible. Delays in collecting debts affect the cash flow of the business and its liquidity. In addition, the risk of uncollectable debts increases as accounts are left to accumulate.

Deal with the tax and insurance of the business
Make provision for tax that must be paid, such as **value-added tax (VAT)**. Also make provision for **income tax**. You may find it very useful to use tax consultants to handle tax affairs for the business.

THE ENTREPRENEURSHIP SERIES

Management for Entrepreneurs

Determine the **insurance needs** of the business and obtain information on how you can make provision for these needs. Use insurance consultants.

1. What are the advantages of a financial policy for your small business?
   ....
   ....
   ....

2. Who does the record-keeping at your business?
   ....

3. What are the possible consequences of a lack of financial planning and control in your business?
   ....
   ....
   ....

4. How would you set about determining the capital need of your business?
   ....
   ....

5. From what internal or external sources do you finance the capital need of your business?
   ....
   ....
   ....

6. What are the negative effects of overdue accounts on your business?
   ....
   ....
   ....

CHAPTER 2
The Financial Function

7. Why should a business insure fixed assets such as buildings, machinery or equipment?

....

....

7 SUMMARY

In this chapter you were introduced to the financial function of the small business. We explained important financial concepts, such as the financial function and financial management.

We discussed the objectives of financial management and saw that in addition to the primary objective of financial management, there are also secondary objectives. We also mentioned and briefly discussed the tasks of financial management. Important aspects of every task were emphasised. Take note of these aspects and ensure that you use them in your business! **If you yourself do not have the expertise to deal with all the financial aspects of your business, enlist the help of experts.** Whatever you do, do not neglect the financial aspects of your small business.

8 SELF-EVALUATION

1. Define the following concepts in one sentence each:

❑ Financial function ....

....

....

❑ Financial management ....

....

....

THE ENTREPRENEURSHIP SERIES
Management for Entrepreneurs

2. Let us now use the case study of the owner of a coffee shop:

   CASE STUDY
   The owner of a coffee shop opened the shop on 1 March with R50 000 capital. She made R250 000 available herself and borrowed the rest (R250 000) from the bank at 15% interest per year. She used part of the money to buy tables and chairs, table-cloths and crockery. The rest of the money she used to buy stock and to finance the operating costs (such as rental, wages and telephone) for the first few months.

   A year later, on 29 February, her books showed that the business produced a net income of R100 000 over the previous 12 months with the capital available to it. During this period, the business paid R30 750 in interest.

   Identify the following concepts in the case study and underline them:
   - Own capital
   - Borrowed capital
   - Fixed capital
   - Working capital
   - Invest
   - Finance
   - Profitability

3. Indicate whether the following statements are true or false:

STATEMENT	TRUE	FALSE
(i) The capital required on an ongoing basis by the business is known as permanent capital.	....	....
(ii) A mortgage bond over 15 years is financed through the money market.	....	....
(iii) Profitability of the enterprise and profitability of own capital are the same.	....	....
(iv) Solvency of the business relates to its ability to make all payments regularly and on time.	....	....
(v) The balance sheet reflects the business's financial position for a certain period.	....	....

CHAPTER 2
The Financial Function

4. Motivate each of your answers in question 3 above in one sentence.

   (i) ....

   (ii) ....

   (iii) ....

   (iv) ....

   (v) ....

5. Use the table below and fill it in for your own small business.

OBJECTIVES OF FINANCIAL MANAGEMENT FOR	
Primary objective	....
Secondary objectives	(i) .... (ii) .... (iii) .... (iv) .... (v) ....

THE ENTREPRENEURSHIP SERIES
Management for Entrepreneurs

6. Explain briefly why each of the following tasks of financial management in the small business must be carried out.

   ❑ Formulation of a financial policy
   ....
   ....

   ❑ Drawing up financial statements
   ....
   ....

   ❑ Financial planning
   ....
   ....

   ❑ Financial control
   ....
   ....

   ❑ Forecast of sales
   ....
   ....

   ❑ Credit evaluations
   ....
   ....

REFERENCE

Kritzinger, A.A.C. & Fourie, J.C.W. 1996. *Basic Principles of Financial Management for a Small Business.* Cape Town: Juta.

3 THE MARKETING FUNCTION

1 LEARNING OBJECTIVES (OUTCOMES)

After you have studied this chapter, you should be able to:

- define the concepts found in marketing;
- explain the marketing process;
- identify and discuss the steps in the marketing plan;
- draw up your own marketing plan.

2 INTRODUCTION

The marketing function in your business is very important. By marketing your products or services you generate an income for your business. You therefore cannot afford to overlook this function. This chapter gives you guidelines on how to handle your marketing.

The small business entrepreneur involved in the day-to-day management of the small business often does not have sufficient time to devote to this function, and may even regard it as a waste of time. But as the business grows and expands, thorough planning, implementation and control of the marketing activities become increasingly important. Naturally, there is also the risk that you will have even less time to devote to this function.

In this chapter we will therefore explain the **marketing process**. In this discussion we will also explain certain **marketing concepts** so that you have a better understanding of the place and role of marketing in your business.

To help you with the marketing of your product or service, the marketing plan will be explained step-by-step with suitable examples.

THE ENTREPRENEURSHIP SERIES
Management for Entrepreneurs

You should therefore be able to draw up your own marketing plan or, if you use a consultant, to have a better understanding of the implications of such a plan.

3 THE MARKETING PROCESS

Irrespective of whether you have a manufacturing business or a small retailing business, marketing is essential to sell your product or service.

> **Marketing** is the transfer of a product or service to the consumer, as well as the activities which make this transfer possible.

To sell your product or service, you must understand your market. You must know who your consumers are, what their needs are and whether your product or service will fulfil their needs. Researching the market is therefore important.

> With **market research** information is gathered on a certain market group so that better marketing decisions can be made. Methods used to obtain this information include interviews, questionnaires and the use of focus groups.

The small business entrepreneur might not always have the time or knowledge to undertake market research. Here are two solutions:

❏ Use a market research company to carry out such a project. The South African Marketing Research Association (SAMRA) can be contacted for suitable referrals.
❏ Internet searches can supply a wealth of information.

Your business is not isolated from its environment. Outside forces have an effect on how your business fares. These factors must therefore be identified. Let us take a simple example.

> The small business entrepreneur has no control over rising interest rates. But what effect do interest rates have on the buying power of consumers? The consumer will have less money to spend.

CHAPTER 3
The Marketing Function

This factor can be regarded either as a threat or as an opportunity by the business, but its effects must be taken into account. Analysis of the environment is therefore very important. When we talk about marketing, we usually refer to this area as the marketing environment. The **marketing environment** is divided into three sub-environments. Within each of these sub-environments, we can identify factors that must be taken into account.

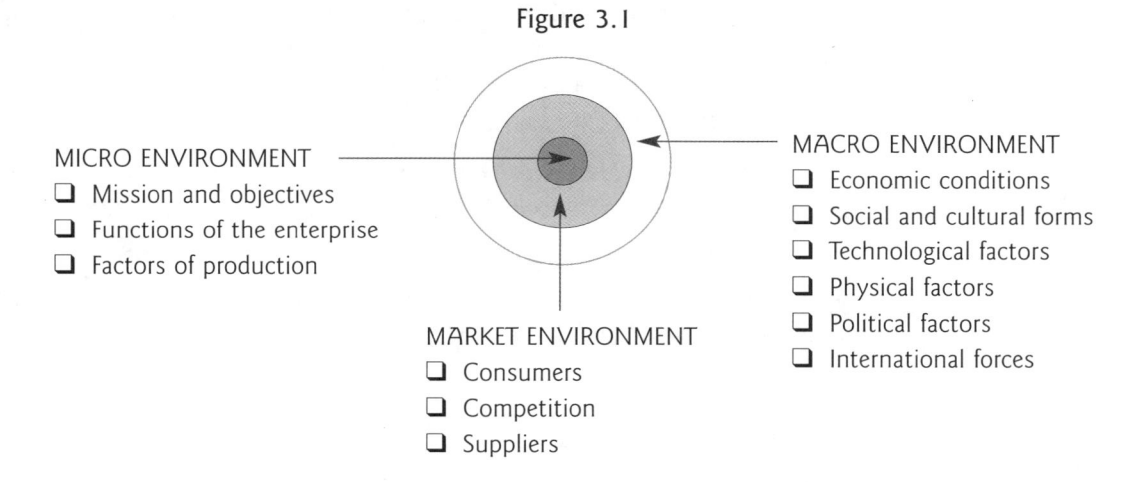

Figure 3.1

MICRO ENVIRONMENT
- Mission and objectives
- Functions of the enterprise
- Factors of production

MACRO ENVIRONMENT
- Economic conditions
- Social and cultural forms
- Technological factors
- Physical factors
- Political factors
- International forces

MARKET ENVIRONMENT
- Consumers
- Competition
- Suppliers

The micro environment
Here we take the internal aspects of the business itself into account. Important factors in this environment are:

❑ **The mission and objectives of the business**
   The mission and objectives state what the business wants to achieve and how it plans to do this.

❑ **The functions of the enterprise**
   The functions of the enterprise refer to all the functions discussed in this book. Marketing is one of these functions.

❑ **Factors of production**
   Factors of production refer to **capital**, such as bank loans when starting the business and machines used in the production process. **Labour** is used to produce the product or offer the service. **Entrepreneurship** refers to the initiative of people such as you who start their own businesses. **Natural resources** are those raw materials provided by nature, such as water and land.

THE ENTREPRENEURSHIP SERIES

Management for Entrepreneurs

An employee at a large firm has made wooden toys on a small scale for young friends and family for a number of years. When he retires, he decides to convert his hobby into a business. He therefore takes the initiative: this displays his **entrepreneurial spirit**. The bank grants him a loan to buy extra woodworking machines. He has now obtained **capital**. He also needs **labour**. Someone must design the toys, while someone else is needed to paint the toys. A cleaner is also required. **Natural resources** used here are primarily wood.

The entrepreneur's **mission** is therefore to make wooden toys of superior quality to meet the needs of the market. His primary **objective** is naturally to make a profit.

To achieve this objective, the entrepreneur must market his wooden toys. **Marketing** is therefore one of the functions that he must keep in mind.

The owner of a business manufacturing paper uses certain factors of production. Place each of the following factors of production under the most suitable heading.

	Labour	Natural resources	Capital
1. Book-keeper			
2. Delivery vehicle			
3. Manager			
4. Paper pulp			
5. Desk			
6. Water			

The market environment

The market environment touches on the macro environment. Main variables in this environment are:

❑ **Consumers and their needs**

This includes all individuals and groups of people who need a product or service and also have the money to buy it.

CHAPTER 3
The Marketing Function

- **Competitors**
  Because you are probably not the only person manufacturing or selling a certain product or service, you should be aware of competitors. Note competitors' prices, their products or services, the way in which they offer their services, and the advertisements and other promotional techniques that they use.

- **Suppliers of resources and services**
  Here we refer, for instance, to those who provide you with certain services or products and so enable you in turn to deliver your product to the consumer. An example of a supplier is Sappi, which provides the wood to manufacturers of wooden furniture.

> The owner of a clothing boutique in a busy shopping centre sells exclusive clothes. There are also branches of three large clothing chain stores in the same shopping centre.
>
> 1. Is it important for the owner of the boutique to study her competitors? Give reasons for your answer.
>
>   ....
>   ....
>   ....
>
> 2. Mention four aspects that the owner of the boutique should note when studying her competitors.
>
>   ....
>   ....
>   ....
>
> The owner of the boutique should note the following:
> Prices, quality, service, product range, target market.

The macro environment

This component involves the market environment as well as the business. In this environment there are various factors that can affect the establishment and prosperity of your business. We can identify the following:

- **Economic factors**
  Factors such as interest rates and exchange rates, inflation and the economic growth rate affect the disposable income of consumers.

❑ **Social and cultural factors**
Here we refer to the demographics of the market. Demographics is the statistical study of a group of people. Here we have to take population growth, geographic location and changes in lifestyle into account.

❑ **Technological factors**
New technology means that new products and services appear and new, improved production methods are used.

❑ **Physical factors**
Physical factors refer to natural resources. Important considerations here are the limited nature of these resources, as well as pollution.

❑ **Political and statutory factors**
Here we refer to the effect of the government and other pressure groups on the business.

❑ **International factors**
Factors beyond the borders of the country also affect the business. Examples are international politics and technology.

Mention only the factor from the macro environment that is involved in the following examples:

EXAMPLE	FACTOR
1. South Africa influenced by land tenure problems in a neighbouring country.	1. ....
2. E-commerce (electronic commerce) becomes the buzzword in business circles.	2. ....
3. Technological developments make the home office a reality.	3. ....
4. The legal issues surrounding e-commerce are very complex.	4. ....
5. Heavy rains influence the supply of natural resources.	5. ....
6. Higher petrol prices increase the prices of products and services.	6. ....

CHAPTER 3
The Marketing Function

From the information above it is clear that not all of these factors apply to all businesses. Nonetheless, they give a clear guideline of how the marketing environment should be analysed.

With this information, and taking the specific resources of your business into account, you can now determine the **market segment** for your specific product or service. From the various market segments you can choose a specific market segment or segments at which you will direct your product or service. This process is known as market segmentation.

> **Market segmentation** is the division of the total market into segments with certain similarities, such as the division of the market into groups of people with the same style of living.

We will explain market segmentation by looking at the following example.

> Suppliers of children's clothes will possibly divide their market into baby clothing, clothing for two-year-olds to ten-year-olds, and clothing for teenagers. From the market segments a target market can be chosen, at which the product or service can be aimed.
>
> ABC Kids' Store, for instance, divides its market into the following market segments:
>
> MARKET SEGMENTS
>
> | Babies |
> | 2–10 years |
> | Teenagers | ← TARGET MARKET
>
> The target market, however, is teenagers.

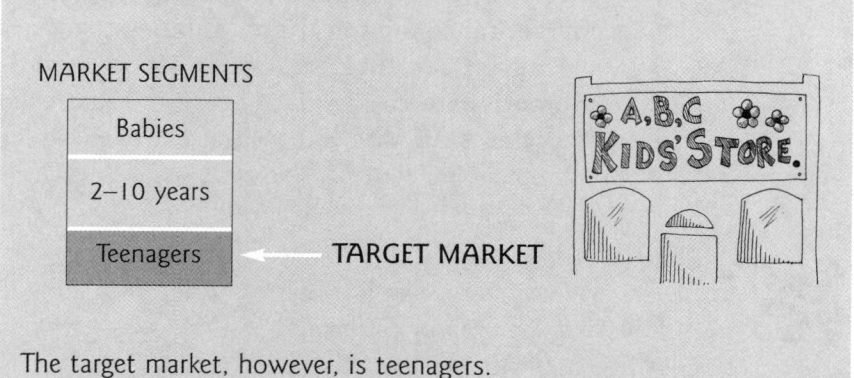

One or more target markets can be chosen, depending on your product or service. ABC Kids' Store, for instance, can focus on the two-year-old to ten-year-old market segment as well as on teenagers. You will now draw up a market presentation for this market segment.

THE ENTREPRENEURSHIP SERIES

Management for Entrepreneurs

The market presentation is known as the marketing mix or marketing strategy and consists of the following:

Figure 3.2

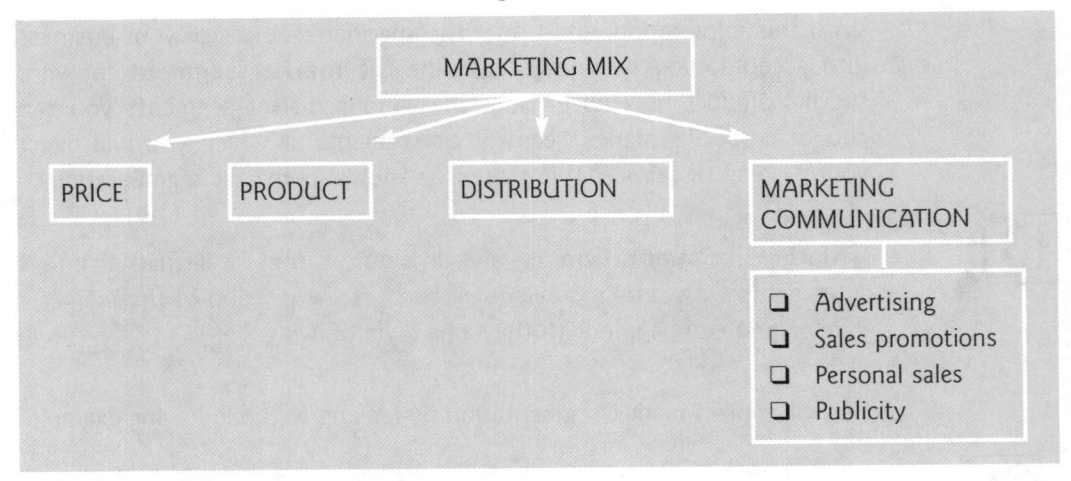

```
                    MARKETING MIX
        ┌──────────┬─────┴─────┬──────────────┐
      PRICE     PRODUCT    DISTRIBUTION    MARKETING
                                         COMMUNICATION
                                         ❏ Advertising
                                         ❏ Sales promotions
                                         ❏ Personal sales
                                         ❏ Publicity
```

❏ **Product:** The product or service that you offer. This includes aspects such as colour, size, packaging and quality.
❏ **Price:** The price that you would ask to reach your profit objective, but also a price that the consumer would be prepared to pay.
❏ **Distribution:** The transfer of products or services from the manufacturer to the consumer, through **intermediaries** (agents).
❏ **Marketing communication:** Marketing communication includes the **advertisements** that you place in various media, **sales promotions** such as special offers, discount coupons and gifts, the **sales staff** that you train and use, and the **publicity** that you obtain from sponsorships, for instance.

A manufacturer makes and sells washing powder for automatic washing machines, packed in plastic containers in sizes of 500 grams or one kilogram. The trademark is clearly indicated on the product with a label.

CHAPTER 3

The Marketing Function

The manufacturer must determine the price of the product. Because many other types of washing powder are available, competitors' prices are very important. However, manufacturers must also take their costs into account.

The product is distributed to all large chain stores, and the manufacturer uses a wholesaler to handle the distribution.

Advertisements are placed in magazines. Discount coupons are also distributed through these magazines.

This is simply a brief explanation of what marketing involves. As the owner of the business, however, you want to know how you can plan, organise and control the marketing function in your business. In the following section we will look at how the **marketing plan** is drawn up.

THE MARKETING PLAN

The **marketing plan** is a detailed plan of how a product or service will be marketed and the time-related details for carrying out the plan.

By drawing up a **marketing plan**, you will:

❑ be able to identify changes in the environment and determine ways of reacting to them;
❑ have a better understanding of the position of your business in the market as regards consumers and competitors;
❑ have a better idea of your objective and how you can achieve it. In other words, you will use your plan as a type of guide or road map to reach your goal;
❑ establish how to obtain resources for your intended plan;
❑ keep staff informed about what is expected of them.

THE ENTREPRENEURSHIP SERIES
Management for Entrepreneurs

> **DO**
>
> Why would you draw up a marketing plan for your business?
> ....
> ....
> ....
> ....

We will now discuss steps used in the marketing plan. You may find that a less formal approach can work better for your business. Remember, however, that the marketing plan must always indicate clearly where you are now, what you are aiming at and how you will achieve it.

To help you with the practical application of the marketing plan, we will refer to examples throughout the text.

> **DO**
>
> The marketing plan consists of the following steps:
> 1. Summary of the intended plan;
> 2. Current marketing position;
> 3. Marketing analysis (SWOT analysis);
> 4. Set objectives;
> 5. Marketing strategy;
> 6. Plan of action;
> 7. Budget;
> 8. Control.

4.1 Summary of the intended plan

As mentioned above, you will also have to submit the plan to other people, such as when you apply for financing. You should therefore start the plan by giving a short summary of exactly what it entails. It should show briefly:

- ❑ what you intend to achieve with the plan;
- ❑ who your target market is;
- ❑ the product or service that you are directing at the target market;
- ❑ what income you expect to make.

Also draw up a table of contents, showing all the points discussed and their page numbers, so that people can easily refer to specific points in the marketing plan.

CHAPTER 3

The Marketing Function

4.2 Current marketing situation

When you analyse your current situation, the following aspects are important:

- First define the current **market segment** at which the product or service is aimed. What is your market segment? What are the trends in that market segment? Is the market segment growing, or is it stagnant or even declining?
- What **products or services** will you offer that market segment? Indicate whether the product is sold regularly, like petrol, which is sold weekly. Also look at whether the product will continue to sell over the long term, or whether demand for the product will pass.
- Study your **competitors**. Remember that there are always competitors in the market. Even if you market a completely new product or service, competitors will quickly enter the market. It is therefore important to know who your direct competitors are. **Direct competitors** refer to businesses that offer the same product or service as you do.
- However, there are also indirect competitors. **Indirect competitors** are those businesses that fulfil the same needs as you do, but with other products or services. The indirect competitor of a business that manufactures curtains, for instance, may be one that manufactures blinds.
- Also study the broader **marketing environment**. Determine, for instance, what technological changes are taking place now that could affect your product or service. Also refer here to our discussion of the marketing environment in section 3.

In the example below we explain these steps and the other steps in the marketing plan.

The owner of a paint shop in Melville, Johannesburg, asked us to analyse the current position in his business.

Market segment:
The market segment is the inhabitants of the immediate Melville area. Because Melville is an old area, people often restore and renovate their houses and they then need paint.

> In addition, the owner also supplies paint to contractors who are not limited to the Melville area. The business delivers the paint to the contractors.
>
> **Product:**
> The product is PVA paint for contractors, including interior and exterior paints.
>
> Colours are mixed in the shop itself.
>
> The business also sells general products, such as paintbrushes.
>
> **Competition:**
> The enterprise is the only paint shop in a 15-km radius. A hardware shop also selling limited quantities of paint opened recently in Melville. However, the owner of the paint shop keeps a greater variety in his shop. Nonetheless, he often finds that customers would like to buy screws and other general hardware when they buy their paint from him.
>
> A variety of factory shops have also opened during the last year. This means that the businesses can now buy their paint direct from the factories. The intermediary can therefore be cut out, but only one brand of paint can be kept in the shops.
>
> **Environmental factors:**
> Consumers often ask whether paint is suitable for use on children's furniture. They want certainty on this point before they use it.

Sales staff must have a broad knowledge of paint techniques so that they can really be of assistance to customers. At the moment they do not have the necessary knowledge.

In the past year there were three increases in the trade prices of paint.

4.3 Marketing analysis (SWOT analysis)

When you have information such as the above on your own business, you can look for the strengths, weaknesses, opportunities and threats to your business. This analysis is known as a SWOT analysis. (The word SWOT is made up of the first letters of the words **s**trengths, **w**eaknesses, **o**pportunities and **t**hreats.) The strengths and weaknesses deal with factors that you can identify in the business itself. The **weaknesses** refer to aspects in business that can improve, and the **strengths** to the advantages that the business has over competitors. **Threats** are factors from outside that could have a negative effect on the business, and **opportunities** can be put to positive use by the business.

Let us look at the paint shop's SWOT analysis.

Weaknesses	**Strengths**
❑ Staff are not well trained ❑ Too few staff to get contract work	❑ Good location ❑ Sufficient capital
Threats	**Opportunities**
❑ Hardware shop ❑ Factory shops	❑ Extension of existing contractors' market ❑ Enter into a contract with a factory to market only its paint and cut out intermediaries

4.4 Set objectives

You should now be able to form a clear picture of what you want to achieve in the marketing of your product or service. This picture should be clearly set out in objectives.

Remember the following requirements of objectives:

❑ Objectives must be **realistic**, and therefore practical and achievable.
❑ They must be **quantifiable**. This means that you must be able to reproduce an objective in figures. These may, for instance, be the percentage by which sales must increase.
❑ They must be linked to a **certain period**.

THE ENTREPRENEURSHIP SERIES

Management for Entrepreneurs

Let us look at how the owner of the paint shop would formulate his objectives.

> ❏ To increase real turnover (that is, the turnover that remains after deducting inflationary increases) by 10% over the next year.
> ❏ To expand the current market by 10% within the next six months through marketing communication.

1. Do the owner's objectives meet the requirements set for objectives? Give reasons for your answer. ....
   ....
   ....

2. What is the first step in the marketing plan?
   ....
   ....

3. Why is it necessary to know who your competitors in the market are?
   ....
   ....

4.5 Marketing strategies (marketing mix)

After you have determined the market situation, done a marketing analysis and set objectives, you need to determine the marketing strategy.

Read through the discussion of the marketing strategy in section 3 again. Now write down all the elements in the marketing strategy:

1. ....
2. ....
3. ....
4. ....

CHAPTER 3
The Marketing Function

How will the owner of the paint shop draw up a marketing strategy for his business?

❑ **Market segment**
The owner will expand the current market segment by stocking additional products such as hardware to meet their needs. He will also expand the current contractors' segment.

❑ **Product**
The owner will negotiate with various factories to obtain a direct supplier. He will then sell only one brand of paint.

Limited quantities of hardware can also be stocked. The shop has sufficient space for this.

❑ **Price**
Prices of paint products can be reduced considerably by cutting out the intermediary. A high percentage of profit can be added to the hardware because it is not the most important line in the shop.

❑ **Distribution**
Sales are made direct from the shop.

If the business purchases an additional vehicle, contractors can be offered a better service.

❑ **Marketing communication**
Advertising: An advertisement currently appears weekly in the *Melville Times*. The owner needs to continue advertising so that consumers are continually reminded about the paint shop.

The owner should also make use of alternative methods of advertising. Three main roads pass through the area. He can find out how many cars use these routes daily and advertise along these routes too.

Sales promotions: Special promotions should be held every three months. The shop should distribute pamphlets every three months, advertising special offers.

> **Publicity:** Offer courses in paint techniques for housewives and others who would like to apply these methods.
>
> **Sales staff:** Train staff in paint techniques. Employ a salesperson who does not want to be involved in the shop but who will concentrate only on contractors.

4.6 Action plan

> The **action plan** is a written plan setting out how an objective in the marketing plan will be accomplished (Ramacitti, 1994:157).

This step is very important. If it is not followed, the marketing plan will be useless. The action plan shows the following:

- The **steps** to be followed;
- The **persons responsible** for carrying out each of the steps;
- The **expected completion date** of each step, showing the expected duration of each step;
- **How** the **success** of the steps will be **measured**.

The paint shop owner's plan of action is divided up as follows:

> - **Product**
>   Negotiate with paint suppliers to obtain only one supplier for the shop. Negotiate with hardware suppliers to open a hardware section in the shop.
>
> - **Prices**
>   Price according to negotiations with suppliers.
>
> - **Distribution**
>   Buy a vehicle.
>
>   Change and adapt the layout of the shop.

CHAPTER 3
The Marketing Function

> ❑ **Marketing communication**
>
> **Advertisements:** Indicate new prices on paint products through advertisements in the newspapers.
>
> Obtain information on prices and draw up outdoor advertisements.
>
> **Sales promotions:** Determine the prices of promotional articles and print and distribute pamphlets with the necessary information.
>
> Decide every three months what products will be on special offer.
>
> **Sales staff:** Arrange a course on paint techniques for sales staff. Appoint a new salesperson and train this person.
>
> The owner must also make certain people responsible for carrying out certain actions. A date must be attached to each of the actions so that the person responsible knows when the action must be completed.

4.7 Budget

A certain amount of funds should already have been allocated in the budget for the marketing of a product or service. In the budget of the business, such an amount is indicated as a total under 'marketing and advertisements', for example. In this step you will now show **how this amount** will be spent on marketing activities **over a certain period**; for instance on advertisements, employee training and sales promotions.

> The owner's plan of action shows how he plans to look at outdoor advertising. He must establish the cost of this first. Next, he must show this as a separate item in the marketing budget. He should also draw up a monthly budget to indicate the planned marketing activities for the year.

75

THE ENTREPRENEURSHIP SERIES

Management for Entrepreneurs

	Budget January 20xx
Marketing method	**Cost**
Outdoor advertising	R800 for 5 spaces
Advertising in the *Melville Times*	R439 for 2 advertisements
Printing of pamphlets	R539 for 10 000 pamphlets
Distribution of pamphlets	R400
Total	R2 178

4.8 Control

Control must now be exercised to ensure that the set objectives are achieved. Control must take place **regularly** because the plans do not make provision for unforeseen circumstances and adjustments that must be made. In this way you can also determine whether the plan of action is a success or not. The paint shop owner, for instance, will study his sales figures to determine whether he has achieved his set objectives or not.

List the steps used in the marketing plan.

1. ....
2. ....
3. ....
4. ....
5. ....
6. ....
7. ....
8. ....

Now draw up a marketing plan for your business. Note the following tips:

CHAPTER 3

The Marketing Function

> ❑ Consultants can be used to help you draw up a marketing plan for your business.
> ❑ Approach institutes such as the Small Business Development Corporation for assistance and information.
> ❑ Use your local newspaper to advertise your product or service. Contact details are usually available in the paper.
> ❑ The Yellow Pages can be used to advertise your business. It can, however, also be used to identify businesses that can help you with your marketing, such as manufacturers and distributors. You will find the contact details in the front of your telephone directory.
> ❑ Use the Internet for online research. Data assist you in decision-making. The Internet can facilitate this process tremendously with the availability of current information.
> ❑ Use the Internet to market your product or service. Internet facilities can be used as a distribution channel, to advertise products and services, for sales promotions such as sampling and contests, to name only a few.

SUMMARY

In this chapter we explained the marketing process. Once you understand this process, you will have a clearer idea of the importance of marketing in the business. We also indicated in our discussion where marketing fits into the business. Certain marketing concepts were explained to help you to draw up a marketing plan.

We looked at the marketing plan as a step-by-step process. The marketing plan, like a road map, serves to guide you to where you want to be and how you should set about getting there. Once you follow these steps, you can draw up a plan of action for marketing your product or service in a practical and structured manner.

SELF-EVALUATION

> 1. Explain (in not more than four lines) why marketing is so important in a business.

THE ENTREPRENEURSHIP SERIES

Management for Entrepreneurs

....
....
....
....

2. You own a small business. Define the following concepts in your own words, indicating what the concepts mean to you as a small business entrepreneur.

   Marketing: ....
   ....

   Market research: ....
   ....

   Market segmentation: ....
   ....

   Marketing strategy: ....
   ....

3. Why is it important to draw up a marketing plan?
   ....
   ....
   ....

Read through the following case study and then answer the questions that follow.

> **Case study: C and G Furniture Dealers**
> C and G Furniture Dealers manufacture tables, chairs, headboards for beds, coffee tables and other wooden items. They make particular use of yellowwood and kiaat. The products and finishes on the furniture are of superior quality. The furniture is therefore expensive and is aimed at the higher income groups. The owner currently markets his products by inserting brochures in magazines. Orders are then taken and made up, and delivered direct to the client.

CHAPTER 3
The Marketing Function

> The owner finds that sales have decreased drastically over the last 12 months. Because he does not have the necessary knowledge of market research, he approaches a consultant to do a research project for him. The findings are summarised as follows:
>
> - Consumers' tastes have changed and they now prefer iron furniture and painted wooden furniture.
> - Consumers find wooden furniture too expensive and select cheaper alternatives.
> - Until now the owner has focused solely on the white market. However, other market segments, such as black consumers, are now expanding.
>
> To add to the owner's problems, wood prices have increased drastically and wood is often not available. He will consequently have to dismiss some of his staff. He would like to avoid this, however, because his artisans are well trained. He decides rather completely to adapt his business.

4. Analyse the owner's current marketing situation.

   Current market segment: ....
   ....
   ....

   Product or service: ....
   ....
   ....

   Competitors: ....
   ....
   ....

   Environmental factors: ....
   ....
   ....

5. Define the principles used in the SWOT analysis.

   Weaknesses ....
   Strengths ....

THE ENTREPRENEURSHIP SERIES

Management for Entrepreneurs

Threats ....
Opportunities ....

6. Do a SWOT analysis for the owner.

WEAKNESSES	STRENGTHS
THREATS	OPPORTUNITIES

7. List the three requirements of objectives.
   ....
   ....
   ....

8. Explain the four elements of the marketing strategy briefly to the owner.
   - ❑ Product: ....
     ....
   - ❑ Price: ....
     ....
   - ❑ Distribution: ....
     ....
   - ❑ Marketing communication: ....

9. Explain the importance of the action plan to the owner.
   ....
   ....
   ....

CHAPTER 3
The Marketing Function

10. What is the purpose of control?

....
....
....

REFERENCES

Carso, D. et al. 1995. *Marketing and Entrepreneurship in SMEs*. Prentice Hall.

Hanson, W. 2000. *Principles of Internet Marketing*. South-Western College Publishing.

Kenny, B. & Dyson, K. 1989. *Marketing in Small Business*. London: Routledge.

Le Roux, E.E. et al. 1999. *Business Management – A Practical and Interactive Approach*. Johannesburg: Heinemann.

Perreault, N.D. & McCarthy, E.J. 2001. *Basic Marketing: A Global-Managerial Approach*. 14th edition. Irwin/McGraw-Hill.

Ramacitti, D.F. 1994. *Do-it-yourself Marketing*. New York: Amacom – American Management Association.

Strauss, J. & Frost, R. 1999. *Marketing on the Internet*. Prentice Hall.

4 THE OPERATIONS FUNCTION

1 LEARNING OBJECTIVES (OUTCOMES)

After you have studied this chapter, you should be able to:

- distinguish between production management and operations management;
- illustrate the transformation process;
- determine the capacity of your business;
- distinguish between the various production systems and decide which will be best for your business;
- identify the factors that affect product design;
- distinguish between aggregate planning, master scheduling and operations scheduling;
- do production planning for your own business;
- distinguish between the various scheduling techniques;
- identify the scheduling technique that will best suit your business.

2 INTRODUCTION

You will remember that in Chapter 1 we mentioned how important it was that every business set objectives and draw up plans to achieve these. The business achieves its objectives through the activities or 'operations' in which it is involved.

Some activities or operations in businesses are concerned with the **manufacture of a product**. Others are concerned with a **supportive role** that eventually makes the manufacture of products possible. Nonetheless, whatever the activities of the business, these activities must

CHAPTER 4
The Operations Function

be **managed** to achieve optimal productivity. South Africa has one of the lowest productivity rates in the world. If these principles of operations management could be more carefully applied, this situation could improve.

In this chapter you will learn the following:

- What is operations management?
- Why is it so important?
- How does operations management affect the small business?
- What effect can operations management have on the productivity of the small business?

PRODUCTION MANAGEMENT VS. OPERATIONS MANAGEMENT

In the past, people used the term **production management** to refer to the management methods and techniques used to manufacture products. However, not all businesses manufacture products; some simply offer a service, such as a banking service, a teaching service or a transport service. To offer this service, however, they must apply a management process that is just as strict as those businesses manufacturing products. Today we use the term **operations management** to describe the management process used in manufacturing organisations as well as in businesses that offer a service. Operations management therefore applies to all businesses and is a wider term than production management.

> **Operations management** is the management of systems or processes that offer products and/or services.

In this chapter we will look more specifically at these systems.

THE ENTREPRENEURSHIP SERIES

Management for Entrepreneurs

DO

List five manufacturing businesses and five businesses that offer a service and briefly give the main objective of each.

MANUFACTURING BUSINESS	OBJECTIVE
Example: Joiner	Manufactures furniture to meet clients' requirements
1.	1. ....
2.	2. ....
3.	3. ....
4.	4. ....
5.	5. ....

SERVICE BUSINESS	OBJECTIVE
Example: Travel agency	Provides a travel and accommodation service
1.	1. ....
2.	2. ....
3.	3. ....
4.	4. ....
5.	5. ....

4 OPERATIONS MANAGEMENT IN THE TRANSFORMATION PROCESS

In any business, whether it manufactures a product or delivers a service, a transformation occurs. **Inputs** (see Chapter 5) are changed (transformed) into **outputs**. In the operations function, these inputs may take the following forms:

- ❏ Money (capital);
- ❏ Manpower (human resources/labour);
- ❏ Machinery;
- ❏ Materials (raw materials and other components).

CHAPTER 4
The Operations Function

These inputs are referred to as 'the four Ms'.

By outputs we mean any product or service that can be sold or exchanged for money (or any other acceptable form of payment). It is these outputs that clients want and that they pay for.

The task of the operations manager (or the owner of the small business) is to ensure that this transformation process runs as smoothly and effectively as possible.

This process can be represented as follows:

INPUTS ⟶ TRANSFORMATION PROCESS ⟶ OUTPUTS

Look at the examples given below to give you a better understanding of the process:

Business	Inputs	Transformation	Outputs
Bakery	Flour, sugar, eggs, yeast, flavourants Ovens and other equipment Bakers (people) Recipes	Mix and mould Bake Food preparation Food packaging	Bread Cakes Pies
Farm	Labour Fields Equipment Seed Fertiliser Animals	Planting Irrigation Harvest	Maize Milk Meat
Hospital	Doctors, nurses, patients Facilities, equipment	Operations Application of knowledge Administration of medicine and therapy	Longer lives Healthy patients Patients return home

THE ENTREPRENEURSHIP SERIES

Management for Entrepreneurs

Now write out the same exercise with any three of the businesses you mentioned on page 85.

Business	Inputs	Transformation	Outputs

Operations management involves the following:

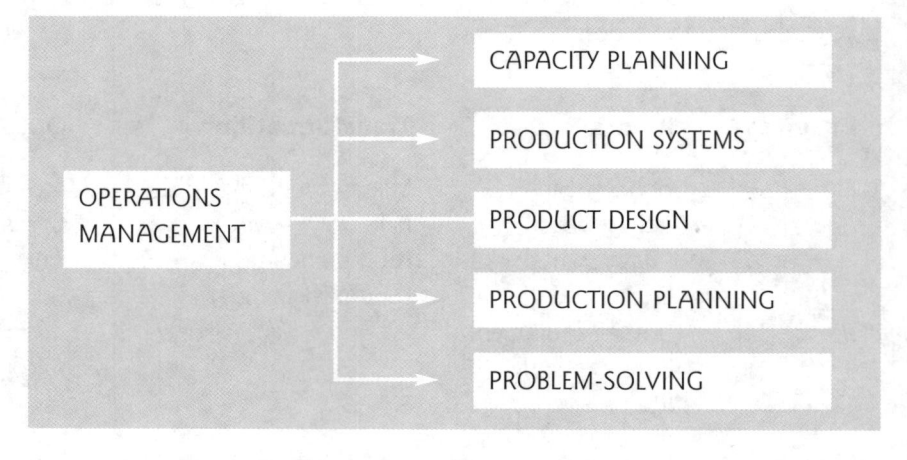

```
                          ┌─→ CAPACITY PLANNING
                          │
                          ├─→ PRODUCTION SYSTEMS
    OPERATIONS            │
    MANAGEMENT   ─────────┼─→ PRODUCT DESIGN
                          │
                          ├─→ PRODUCTION PLANNING
                          │
                          └─→ PROBLEM-SOLVING
```

We will explain operations management throughout this chapter on the basis of the following example.

As a hobby, a joiner makes Cape Dutch furniture from exotic timbers such as blackwood, yellowwood and stinkwood. He first made them just for his own use. However, because he set high standards and practised good workmanship, his friends were impressed with his furniture and started placing orders with him.

CHAPTER 4

The Operations Function

A local furniture dealer also saw the joiner's products and drew up a contract with him to manufacture certain items exclusively for his dealership.

As a result of the increase in sales, the joiner will naturally now be busier than ever before. Until now, he has done his joinery after hours because he also had a full-time job. Now, however, he may reconsider the situation. There are many decisions he will have to take. He may need extra help, and if so, how many people should he appoint? Does he have enough equipment to meet all his orders?

5 CAPACITY PLANNING

In our example above, the decisions that the joiner must take are decisions on **capacity planning**. The capacity of a business can be described as follows:

> The **capacity** of a business is the greatest possible workload that a business can handle within a certain period.

If a business wishes to function effectively, it must plan its capacity. The small businessperson must therefore calculate her/his maximum output, or the maximum output of her/his various operations units. An operations unit may be a machine, a group of machines, or a group of workers with or without machines. Let us look at an example.

> The joiner calculates that he can manufacture a maximum of 10 coffee tables per month. If he gets an order for 20 coffee tables per month, he will therefore have to appoint at least one other joiner who can work at the same pace as he does.

However, there are other factors to be taken iʳ account. The joiner does not only make coffee t He also makes other products such as tra· stands and beds.

To determine the quantity of workerˢ he will need, he must determine tʰ that it takes to manufacture ⸺

many ways in which standard times can be calculated. However, the joiner decides to record the time that he spends on average in manufacturing an item. This will give him an indication of the standard time. Once he has manufactured a good quantity of every item, he calculates the following **average times**:

Coffee table	–	8 hours
Tray	–	3 hours
Hall-stands	–	24 hours

Building on this calculation, the joiner must now determine how many sales he will have in a month.

The sales budget is a **forecast of the planned or expected sales in the next year**, and is calculated using specific forecasting techniques. Because the joiner's business is still small, he will probably not need to use specialised forecasting techniques. However, once his business starts to grow, he will have to look at such techniques to eliminate uncertainties about future sales. Various books give details on these techniques, including Stevenson (mentioned at the end of this chapter).

The joiner draws up the following **forecast** for his sales for the month:

Coffee tables	–	20
Trays	–	30
Hall-stands	–	4

Total work in hours can therefore be converted as follows:

Coffee tables	–	20 × 8 hours	=	160 hours
Trays	–	30 × 3 hours	=	90 hours
Hall-stands	–	4 × 24 hours	=	96 hours

Total working hours for the month are therefore 346 hours.

Continuing from here, assume that the joiner plans to have his workers (whom he must still appoint) work a 9-hour working day: from 08:00 to 17:00. However, he allows two tea-times of 15 minutes each and half an hour for lunch. **Effective working time** that he expects from each worker is therefore:

9 hours – (half an hour for teas and half an hour for lunch) = 8 hours

CHAPTER 4
The Operations Function

In addition, assume that every worker will work a five-day working week; usually 22 days per month. The **total available and effective time** (per month) that the joiner expects from every worker is therefore:

22 x 8 = 176 hours

We can now easily **calculate the amount of workers** that the joiner will have to appoint to accommodate the work for the month:

Amount of work (in hours) per month   =   346 hours
Number of hours available per worker   176 hours

                                                       =   1,9 workers

The joiner must therefore appoint two workers to handle the workload for the following month.

In the same way you can calculate the capacity of every machine used in your production process.

> Now use the above method to calculate the capacity of the following work stations:
>
> Machine 1:   Output capacity per hour = 12 units
> Machine 2:   Output capacity per hour = 20 units
>
> Available machine time: Both machines are tended by one of four possible operators. If an operator cannot be with a machine, the machine is turned off. Every operator starts working at 08:00 and working time ends at 16:00. In between, each operator can have 15 minutes for tea and 1 hour for lunch every day. Assume that there are 22 working days in the month.
>
> 1. Calculate the machine capacity per month.
>   ....
>   ....
>   ....
>   ....

2. Calculate the labour capacity for the month.

   ....
   ....
   ....
   ....

6 PRODUCTION SYSTEMS

In the previous section we saw how the joiner calculated the capacity of his business. However, this does not mean that he cannot improve on this capacity. He should look at whether he can manufacture the products **faster** and **more effectively**. If so, he may be able to employ fewer people and use fewer machines. The joiner therefore decides to investigate the method of manufacture – the production system – to find a better, more productive method of production.

There are three main types of production systems:

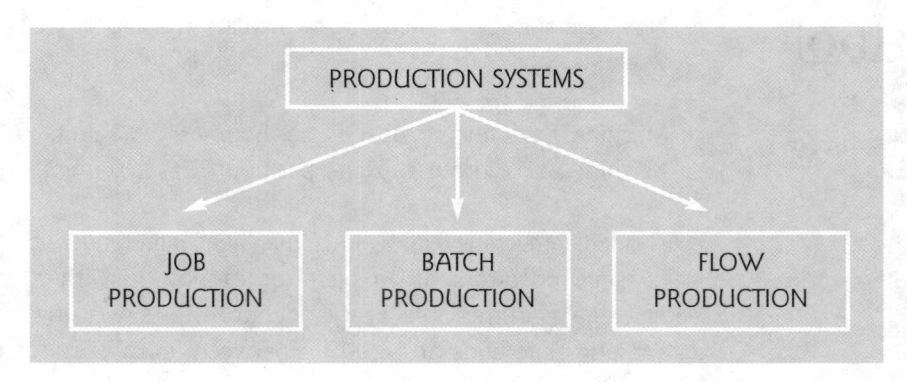

```
                    PRODUCTION SYSTEMS
                   /        |        \
              JOB         BATCH        FLOW
          PRODUCTION   PRODUCTION   PRODUCTION
```

We will now explain each of these production systems briefly using the example of the joiner's business.

6.1 Job production

Small businesses often use this type of production system because it involves product manufacture or service according to the **needs and/or designs of the client**. A prospective client will therefore request the joiner to make a unique coffee table designed by the client (usually a few

CHAPTER 4
The Operations Function

ideas put down on paper and explained to the manufacturer). It is highly unlikely that the joiner will again have to make such a coffee table, and the complete production process must therefore be adjusted to manufacture this table.

Because the coffee table consists of various components, the joiner will have to adjust the machines a couple of times to manufacture every part. Production time on this specific table will therefore be much longer. Remember, though, that the joiner's time will be measured directly in the price of the table. This coffee table will therefore be fairly expensive.

Other examples of work according to the job production system are the building of a house, a bridge or a boat.

6.2 Batch production

Assume the joiner likes the table the client designed, and that the client has no objection to the joiner manufacturing the table in **bulk batches**. The joiner realises that he can increase his productivity if he reduces the amount of time spent adjusting the machines. By grouping the operations, therefore, he could possibly manufacture six tables in the time that it took him to manufacture two on the job production system.

The joiner will therefore adjust the saw once and saw all the parts (enough for six tables) at once. He will then adjust the planer and plane all the parts together. He will continue in this way until all the parts have been manufactured and he can simply put them all together.

What is important in this type of production is that the parts must be well **specified** and **standardised**. For instance, all the table legs must look exactly the same and be made according to the same specifications. It therefore means also that the parts must be well designed. Most manufacturers in South Africa and in the rest of the world work according to this production system.

91

There are better systems to use than batch production, but these are often not used because they are not known. If you wish to know more about them, read up on 'group technology'. At the end of this chapter we recommend Burbridge, which is a good source on this.

6.3 Flow production

The entrepreneur in our example will probably never need this system because it is **extremely repetitive** and manufactures **highly standardised parts.** A typical example of flow production is the production found at a business such as SASOL, which manufactures only one type of product, such as an oil or a chemical, for weeks at a time. When a different product must be manufactured, all the machines in the factory must be switched off and the production lines cleaned. The term used here is 'shutdown'.

If the joiner uses this system, he will allocate certain machines to manufacture only certain parts all the time.

The greatest advantage of such a system is that the machines are set only once to manufacture a large number of parts or products.

In a small business it would generally be advisable first to look at job production and then, if demand grows, to implement batch production.

1. Will a product manufactured according to the job production system be more expensive or cheaper than one manufactured by batch production? Give reasons for your answer.

   ....
   ....
   ....

2. When would you switch from job production to batch production?

   ....
   ....
   ....

CHAPTER 4
The Operations Function

3. Why would a business manufacturing cardboard boxes of various sizes for packaging use flow production? Give two reasons.

....

....

....

PRODUCT DESIGN

Figure 4.1

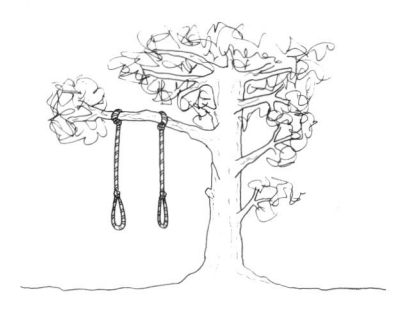

What the client would have liked   *What the client received*

The entrepreneur now decides to use the batch production system. However, one of the requirements of such a system is that the parts are well-planned and well-defined or standardised.

When choosing and designing the product, the entrepreneur should be guided by the consumer. Sometimes, through advertising and research, the entrepreneur guides the consumer (this happened, for instance, in the case of the cellular telephone). Remember, the product is the key to your business's existence, and the success of the business depends on whether the **product or service is acceptable to the client**. If the product is much in demand, sales will be high and production will also be high.

From time to time it is necessary to design or redesign a product. Taste and preference differ and change continually. Look again at the chapter on marketing, which also looks at the effect of changes in consumer needs.

At this point we will assume that the product idea already exists and has been investigated for viability and marketability. The product must now be designed for manufacture.

THE ENTREPRENEURSHIP SERIES

Management for Entrepreneurs

> **NB** Take the following factors into account in the design of a product or service for your business:
>
> - Use or function;
> - Sales appearance;
> - Design effectiveness;
> - Raw materials;
> - Simplification;
> - Determining of costs;
> - Patents and patent law;
> - Consumer complaints;
> - Inquiries and after-sales service.

7.1 Use or function

Design must always focus on the eventual use of a product. It must therefore always fulfil the function for which it will be used.

7.2 Sales appearance

You will understand that a product must look good in order to sell. If the product does not look good, prospective clients will not even consider it. Often the sales appearance is more important than the product's function: think of an item of clothing as an example. Appearance includes packaging and presentation of the product on the shelf. Who will buy a product packaged in a torn cardboard box that clearly got wet at some stage?

7.3 Design effectiveness

Proper, effective design ensures that the product is user-friendly and fit for the purpose for which it is sold. A good way of testing whether the product is indeed effective is to use it yourself, or to give a few (about 10) away free to typical consumers and to ask them to point out weaknesses in the design to you. As a reward you may let them keep the test model, plus a unit of the new, improved design.

CHAPTER 4
The Operations Function

7.4 Raw materials

Consider carefully the advantages and disadvantages of the various options under raw materials. We will take the example of furniture. If the joiner must choose between pine furniture (which is fairly inexpensive) and stinkwood furniture (an expensive but more durable wood), he would ask: 'Who will buy this furniture?' The answer to this question will determine what type of wood he will use.

7.5 Simplification

Designers must try to use standardised parts in designing a product. Take, for instance, the making of shoes. Manufacturers can literally make a shoe for every individually sized foot, but this will not be cost-effective. They therefore concentrate on the manufacture of standardised sizes. Some even limit themselves to manufacturing only the most common sizes.

7.6 Determining of costs

Most products are highly competitive. A product must therefore not be too expensive to compete with others, or it will not sell. Even though the product may be completely new on the market and not have any competitors, the price should not be too high or it will frighten off potential buyers.

7.7 Patents and patent law

Be very careful to check that the design has not already been patented. If it has, this may give rise to a lawsuit, which will have major cost implications.

Consider the Patents Act 57 of 1978 before you introduce a 'new' product to the market.

7.8 Consumer complaints

Consumers will bring your attention to weaknesses in your product in the form of complaints. Investigate all complaints and change the design where necessary.

Always try to improve on your service and your product. Look at the quality of the product as well as the extent to which it achieves the purpose for which it was designed.

7.9 Inquiries and after-sales service

South Africa must be one of the countries with the poorest after-sales service in the world. Yet this is one of the most important service aspects, because it can ensure a business's success. Poor after-sales service results in loss of clients, while good after-care will win you more clients.

A good way of bringing the attention of clients to your after-sales service is to offer some tangible reward. Think of something original. For instance, if you are a car dealer, you may give your clients a 'lifelong service manual', or if you are a jeweller, you may give a voucher for the first free restringing of a new pearl necklace.

> **Practical tips for designing a product or service**
> Always consider the **client**: is the product that you designed what the client had in mind?
>
> Ensure that the **appearance of the product** is acceptable to the client. The design of the product may fulfil the function for which it was designed, but if it is unattractive (or consumers do not accept it for some other reason), sales of the product will be seriously affected.
>
> If you use batch production and normally manufacture a prototype of the final product, make certain that the **design is factory-friendly**, or that it can easily be manufactured in bulk in a factory. It is a good idea to try a small production run and to clear up any problems that may occur immediately.

CHAPTER 4
The Operations Function

> Involve the **production staff** in the product at the design stage too. Early contributions from their side can save much trouble later on.
>
> **Quality control** must be applied at every stage of manufacture, to every part of the product. Once the product has been fully manufactured, it is too late to apply quality control, because much cost has then already gone into the various stages of manufacture.

1. Why is the appearance of an article for sale so important?
   ....
   ....
   ....
   ....

2. What should you take into account when deciding on a raw material for your product?
   ....
   ....
   ....
   ....

3. How does a simple design affect the cost of manufacture?
   ....
   ....
   ....
   ....

4. What are the benefits of consumer complaints on the design of a product?
   ....
   ....
   ....
   ....

8 PRODUCTION PLANNING

In this section we will look at:

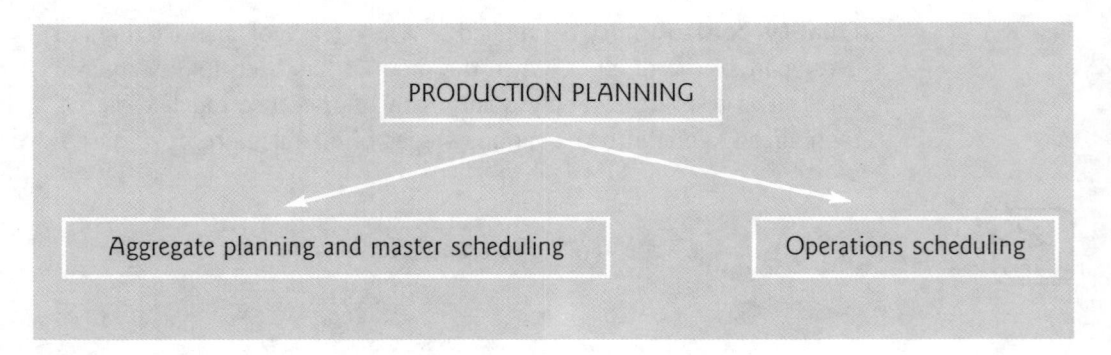

```
                    PRODUCTION PLANNING
                   ↙                    ↘
Aggregate planning and master scheduling    Operations scheduling
```

We will also give you certain guidelines for planning and scheduling the operations in your business.

8.1 Aggregate planning and master scheduling

The **aggregate plan** for a business indicates what **product groups or families** the business **should manufacture**. For instance, the joiner may indicate in his aggregate plan that he plans to manufacture the following quantities of his three products during the coming year:

Coffee tables	–	240
Trays	–	360
Hall-stands	–	48

The aggregate plan is usually drawn up for a period of between 3 and 18 months in advance. This plan is also derived from the sales plan.

The **master schedule** (also called the master production schedule) usually indicates the **planned production per time interval**. For instance, the joiner may decide to make coffee tables at a fixed rate of production of 20 per month; trays at varying rates (as required by demand); and hall-stands at a fixed rate of four per month.

CHAPTER 4
The Operations Function

His plan will therefore be more or less as follows:

MASTER SCHEDULE — Aggregate plan

PRODUCT	JAN	FEB	MAR	APR	MAY	JUN	JUL	AUG	SEP	OCT	NOV	DEC	TOTAL	
Coffee tables	20	20	20	20	20	20	20	20	20	20	20	20	240	← Fixed rate
Trays	20	20	20	35	40	50	50	40	35	25	15	10	360	← Fixed rate
Hall-stands	4	4	4	4	4	4	4	4	4	4	4	4	48	← Fixed rate

The joiner can now determine his production schedule for every week, and eventually every day, on this basis.

Remember: Do your planning YOURSELF, because if someone else does it for you, it will not meet all your specific requirements.

8.2 Operations scheduling

Operations scheduling refers to the determination of the sequence in which jobs and activities are to be completed in the manufacturing plant (De Wit & Hamersma, 1992:275).

In this section we will discuss only the rules of priority of scheduling techniques. These techniques are used to determine in which sequence products should be manufactured or clients served. The techniques are relatively simple, and you will have to decide which will best suit your business.

Figure 4.2

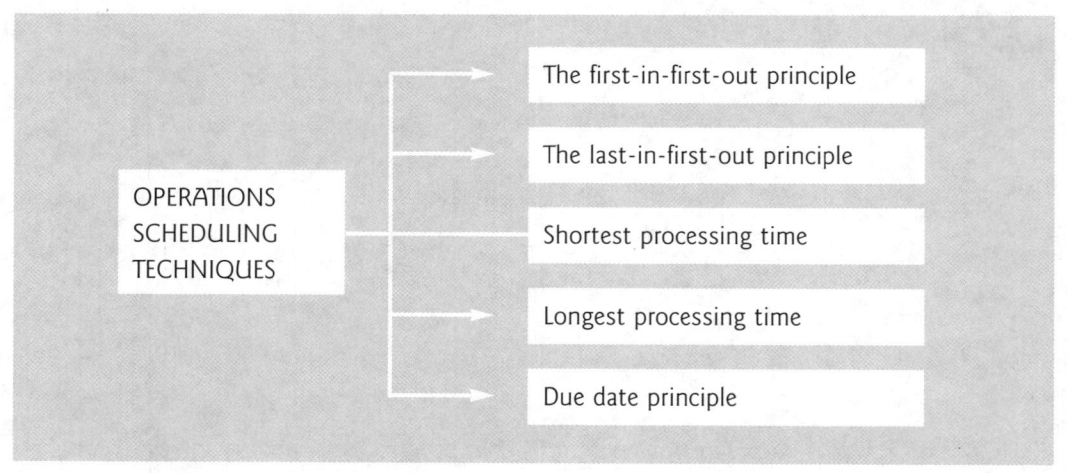

```
                          ┌─→ The first-in-first-out principle
                          │
                          ├─→ The last-in-first-out principle
   OPERATIONS             │
   SCHEDULING   ──────────┼─→ Shortest processing time
   TECHNIQUES             │
                          ├─→ Longest processing time
                          │
                          └─→ Due date principle
```

The first-in-first-out (FIFO) principle

According to this principle, products which are required first are manufactured first, or clients standing at the front of the queue are served first.

The last-in-first-out (LIFO) principle

In this system the product required last is manufactured first, or the client who arrived last is served first. However, very few businesses use this system.

Shortest processing time

Here the product with the shortest processing time is manufactured first, and the product with the longest processing time is manufactured last.

CHAPTER 4
The Operations Function

Longest processing time
The product with the longest processing time is manufactured first.

Due date principle
The product that **MUST** be ready first according to the sequence of orders is manufactured first.

In highly specialised businesses, computers are used to do such scheduling, to ensure that the products can be completed with the shortest total waiting time for the series as a whole.

You may combine one or more of these methods, or formulate other methods based on aspects such as the relative importance of the client, the size of the order or the availability of raw materials or resources.

If you wish to know more about scheduling techniques, look at the book by Stevenson that we recommend at the end of this chapter.

1. Answer the following questions by filling in the missing words.

    (a) Production planning involves aggregate planning, ... and ....

    (b) A .... indicates the intended rate at which products will be manufactured.

    (c) An aggregate plan indicates what .... or product families a business plans to manufacture.

    (d) .... indicates the sequence in which tasks and activities should take place in the production process.

2. Which scheduling techniques would you use in your business? Give reasons for your choice.

    ....
    ....
    ....
    ....
    ....

9 PROBLEM-SOLVING

If your product is well marketed and well manufactured and there is a real need in the market, your business should quickly grow. However, problems could arise about capacity in the business, as regards resources (human resources or manpower, material, money, machines) as well as space. As demand increases you will have to produce more, but this also means that you will have to spend more.

Often businesses actually do have the capacity to produce more, but as a result of mismanagement the capacity is not utilised to the full. The following factors are involved here:

- Poor time management;
- Unproductive methods of manufacture;
- Incorrect scheduling;
- Efforts to please each client at all costs, at the expense of other clients or the business itself.

You can solve these problems by following the guidelines below.

Poor time management
This problem is often found with the more senior staff at a business. There simply never seems to be enough time in a day to get everything done! Here we can recommend that you attend a course on time management or read a good book on the topic.

Manage your time effectively, for instance, by setting yourself six jobs per day that you feel are the most important. Then prioritise these jobs again in order of importance and carry them out in this order.

Unproductive methods
Start at the beginning of the production process and determine where the process is held up or where the bottleneck occurs. Investigate the operations carried out here, and try to speed things up by developing more productive methods. Any improvement here will improve total output.

Incorrect scheduling
Ensure that your schedules are realistic. Allow enough time for every operations activity, and also allow enough time before, between and

CHAPTER 4
The Operations Function

after the activities. Don't schedule the whole capacity of the plant, because enough time should be allowed for changes and emergencies. Allow workers or operators to assume responsibility for keeping to the schedule.

Efforts to satisfy clients at all costs

Entrepreneurs must ask themselves whether they will satisfy each client, potentially at the expense of another, or whether they will be open with clients and clearly say when orders may be late.

Whatever is decided, keep to it. Ensure, however, that you can justify the decision to other clients.

1. Write down the missing words in the empty spaces.

   Businesses often do not use their full capacity as a result of problems such as:

   PROBLEMS

(a)	(b)	(c)	(d)
....	....	....	Efforts always to satisfy clients

2. Do you have a solution to each of the above problems? Write each down in the spaces provided:

   (a) ....

   (b) ....

   (c) ....

   (d) ....

THE ENTREPRENEURSHIP SERIES
Management for Entrepreneurs

10 SUMMARY

Operations management involves transforming inputs ('the four Ms') through a variety of production systems (job production, batch or flow production) so as eventually to get a usable and saleable product or service. The product must be designed in such a way that it is easy to manufacture and will be in demand on the market. A smooth transformation process also requires careful planning. We start with an aggregate plan, which is refined into a daily scheduling of tasks. Various techniques may be applied to overcome the problem of insufficient capacity.

Operations management is a dynamic discipline. It requires integration of various activities and processes to ensure products or services of high quality. With the lifting of sanctions, South African businesses found themselves in an increasingly competitive environment. Effective operations management can ensure that your business is profitable and keeps up with the market.

11 SELF-EVALUATION

1. What aspects should you pay attention to with the management of the operations function?

CHAPTER 4
The Operations Function

2. Complete the following diagram by writing in the missing words.

```
..................  →  TRANSFORMATION  →  ..................
                         PROCESS
         ↓                                    ↓
   ❑ ............                       ❑ Product
   ❑ ............                         or
   ❑ ............                       ❑ ............
   ❑ Raw materials
```

3. Explain the transformation process in your own (or your intended) business. (First indicate whether it is a manufacturing or a service business. Also indicate what inputs you will use, what transformation occurs and what outputs you produce.)

Type of business	Inputs	Transformation	Outputs

4. What word from column B best suits the description in column A? Write down only the letter as your answer.

A	B
1. It may be a machine, a group of machines or a group of workers with or without machines. Answer:	(a) Effective working time
2. The average time that it takes to manufacture one item. Answer:	(b) Flow production

THE ENTREPRENEURSHIP SERIES
Management for Entrepreneurs

3. This production system involves manufacture or service according to the needs or design of the client. Answer:	(c) Capacity planning
4. This indicates the total available working time of a worker. Answer:	(d) Job production
5. This production system is used mainly to manufacture highly standardised parts year in and year out. Answer:	(e) An operations unit
6. This involves determining the greatest or most productive workload that an operations unit can handle. Answer:	(f) Batch production
7. This production method is used to increase the productivity of an operations unit where items are manufactured in bulk. Answer:	(g) Standard time

5. List all the aspects that should be kept in mind in the design of a product.

   ❏ .... ❏ ....
   ❏ .... ❏ ....
   ❏ .... ❏ ....
   ❏ .... ❏ ....
   ❏ .... ❏ ....

CHAPTER 4
The Operations Function

6. Assume you are the owner of a manufacturing business. Indicate what product(s) you manufacture and how many you intend to manufacture in the next year (aggregate plan). Also indicate which products you would manufacture at a varying rate and which at a fixed rate (master schedule). Use the following table to help you with your production planning.

PRODUCT	JAN	FEB	MAR	APR	MAY	JUN	JUL	AUG	SEP	OCT	NOV	DEC	TOTAL	RATE (Variable or fixed)

Quantity to be produced

7. (a) List five scheduling techniques.
   ❏ ....
   ❏ ....
   ❏ ....
   ❏ ....
   ❏ ....

   (b) Which technique(s) would you use to manufacture the product(s) you indicated in question 6? Give reasons for your answer.

   ....
   ....
   ....
   ....
   ....

12 REFERENCES

Buffa, E.S. & Sarin, R.K. 1987. *Modern Production/Operations Management.* 8th edition. New York: John Wiley & Sons.

De Wit, P.W.C. & Hamersma, S.A. 1992. *Production and Operations Management – A Practical Approach.* Johannesburg: Southern.

Naylor, J. 1996. *Operations Management.* London: Pitman.

Stevenson, W.J. 1995. *Production/Operations Management.* 5th edition. Homewood, Illinois: Irwin.

RECOMMENDED BOOKS

If you wish to do further reading on operations management, we can recommend the following books:

Burbridge, J.L. 1975. *The Introduction of Group Technology.* Butler & Tanner.

De Wit, P.W.C. & Hamersma, S.A. 1992. *Production and Operations Management – A Practical Approach.* Johannesburg: Southern.

Stevenson, W.J. 1995. *Production/Operations Management.* 5th edition. Homewood, Illinois: Irwin.

5 THE PURCHASING FUNCTION

1 LEARNING OBJECTIVES (OUTCOMES)

After you have studied this chapter, you should be able to:

- give a brief explanation of the role and importance of the purchasing function in the small business;
- discuss the objectives of the purchasing function with specific reference to the difference between broad, long-term objectives and short-term objectives;
- discuss the activities of the purchasing function and apply them in your business;
- discuss the management of purchasing with specific reference to:
  - planning purchasing;
  - organising purchasing;
  - the control of purchasing.

2 INTRODUCTION

Entrepreneurs usually establish small businesses with one aim in mind: to make a profit so as to provide a living for themselves. They make this profit by supplying consumers with products and/or services in exchange for some of the consumers' disposable income.

To deliver the business's product or service, the entrepreneur needs inputs like capital, labour, raw materials, parts (components) and other resources. Capital is provided by the financial function and labour by the human resource (personnel) function. The raw materials, parts and other resources are the responsibility of the **purchasing function**. Henceforth we will refer to these factors (raw materials, parts and other resources) as **means of production** or **production means**.

Figure 5.1

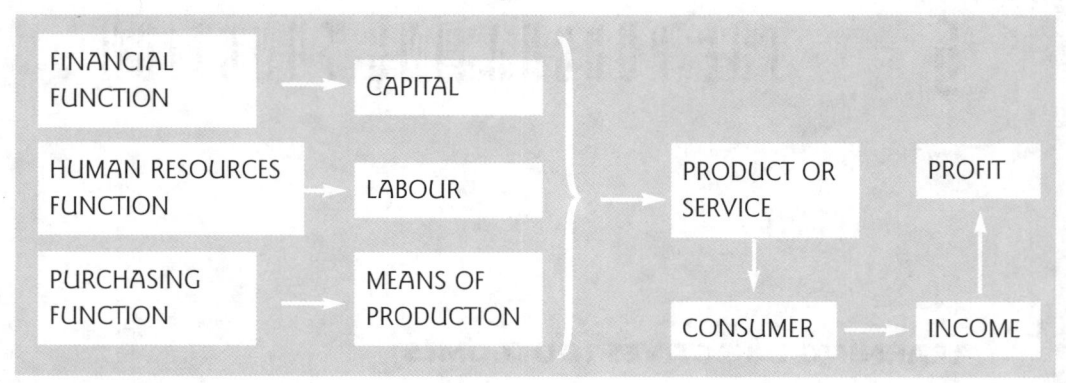

```
FINANCIAL
FUNCTION           →   CAPITAL
                                          ⎫
HUMAN RESOURCES                           ⎬  →  PRODUCT OR    →   PROFIT
FUNCTION           →   LABOUR             ⎭      SERVICE           ↑
                                                    ↓
PURCHASING             MEANS OF
FUNCTION           →   PRODUCTION              CONSUMER   →   INCOME
```

In this chapter we will look at the role, importance and functioning of purchasing in the small business. We will look specifically at the **objectives** of the purchasing function, its **activities** and its **management**.

3 THE ROLE AND IMPORTANCE OF THE PURCHASING FUNCTION IN THE SMALL BUSINESS

As we mentioned above, the purchasing function must ensure that the business acquires **all the means of production** necessary for the production process or for providing a service.

The role of the purchasing function in the business can be defined as follows:

> The **purchasing function** must ensure that production means of the right quality are supplied to the business in the right quantities, at the right time, to the right place, from the right suppliers at the right price.

In this chapter we will discuss the various components of this definition. These are:

- quality;
- quantity;
- timing;
- price;
- suppliers;
- place.

CHAPTER 5

The Purchasing Function

By this time you are probably aware of the fact that the various functions in your small business are interdependent. If the purchasing function does not fulfil its responsibilities, the other functions or departments in the business cannot function at their optimum levels. The operations function and the marketing function in particular are affected if production means of the right quality are not available on time in the right place. The production process can be brought to a halt and orders will then not be delivered on time. In section 4 we explain how problems such as these threaten the profitability, and even the very existence, of the business.

Manufacturing businesses spend more than half of their income from sales on production means. This emphasises the importance of the purchasing function, because the **cost of production means** has a real effect on the **profitability** of the business. We will explain this as follows: means of production contribute directly to the cost of the final product. The selling price is calculated by taking the cost of the product (including the cost of production means) and placing a percentage profit on top of that. If the purchasing function can save costs, the overall costs in the business are lower and it therefore makes a bigger profit (if selling prices remain constant). However, the opposite is also true, as you can see from the diagram that follows.

Figure 5.2

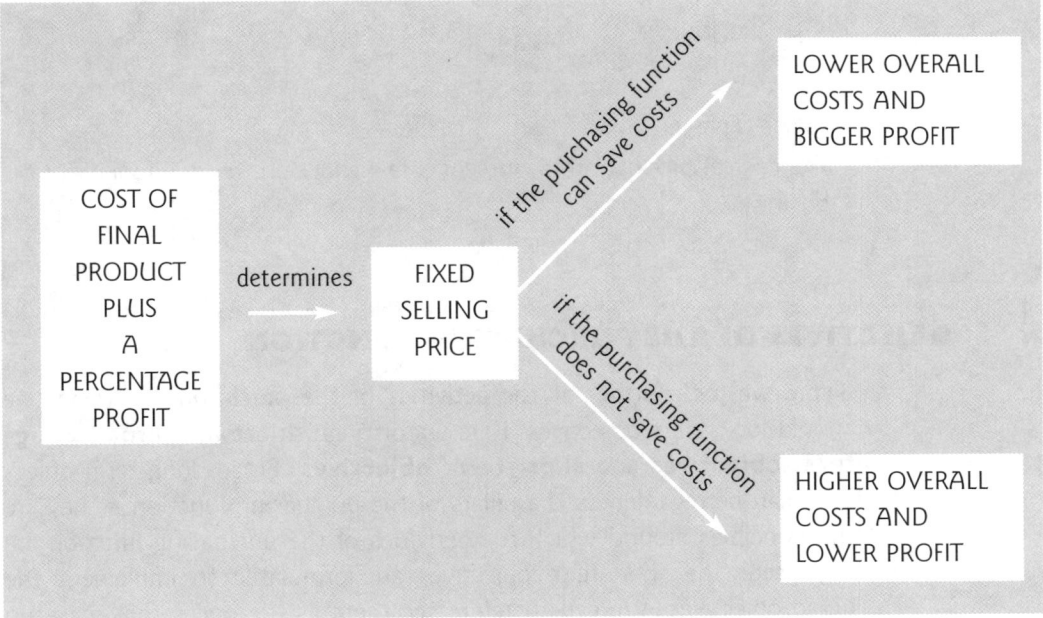

COST OF FINAL PRODUCT PLUS A PERCENTAGE PROFIT → determines → FIXED SELLING PRICE

if the purchasing function can save costs → LOWER OVERALL COSTS AND BIGGER PROFIT

if the purchasing function does not save costs → HIGHER OVERALL COSTS AND LOWER PROFIT

The activities of the purchasing function therefore directly affect the profitability of the small business.

eg Assume you are the owner of a business that makes shoes. Normal production cost per pair is R80,00. The consumer is prepared to pay R120,00 for the shoes, and your price is therefore fixed. The profit per pair will therefore be R40,00 (33,3% of the selling price).

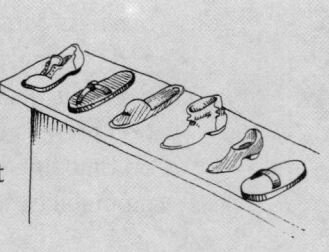

Now look at the effect that increased and reduced costs have on your profit margin:

	Normal cost	Higher cost	Lower cost
SELLING PRICE	R120	R120	R120
COST PER PAIR	R80	R100	R70
PROFIT	R40	R20	R50
% PROFIT: SELLING PRICE	33,3%	16,7%	41,7%

CONCLUSION:
The cost of production means has a real effect on the profitability of a business.

4 OBJECTIVES OF THE PURCHASING FUNCTION

Before we look further at the activities of the purchasing function, we should look at its objectives. Here we distinguish between **broad, long-term objectives** and **short-term objectives**. Broad, long-term objectives can be regarded as the pillars of the purchasing function – they are the principles around which the activities of the purchasing function are organised. The short-term objectives are formulated to implement the broad objectives. We can therefore see them as the bricks that make up

CHAPTER 5

The Purchasing Function

each pillar. These objectives indicate what must be done in the short term (usually a year) to achieve the broad, long-term objectives. Due dates are usually determined for each short-term objective.

Figure 5.3

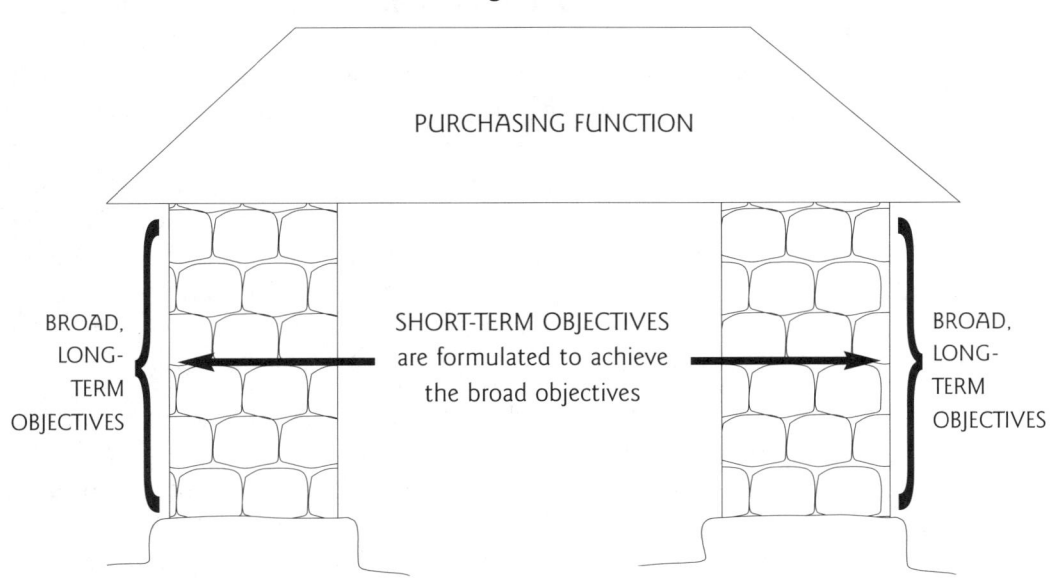

PURCHASING FUNCTION

BROAD, LONG-TERM OBJECTIVES

SHORT-TERM OBJECTIVES are formulated to achieve the broad objectives

BROAD, LONG-TERM OBJECTIVES

NB **Over the long term, the purchasing function tries to achieve the following broad objectives:**

BROAD, LONG-TERM OBJECTIVES

- CONTINUITY
- QUALITY
- EFFECTIVE MANAGEMENT OF STOCK
- ALTERNATIVE SUPPLIERS
- GOOD RELATIONS WITH SUPPLIERS
- GOOD RELATIONS WITH OTHER FUNCTIONS IN THE BUSINESS

Continuity

The aim of the purchasing function is to make the right production means available in the right place and at the right time so that the **production process** can continue **without stopping**.

It is important for the **right production means** to be delivered at the **right time**. Production means that are delivered too late can cause a delay in the production process and thus unnecessary costs for the business. If a small business follows the just-in-time approach, it means that it always receives its stock just in time for production and produces its products just in time for delivery to the client. If the supplier therefore delivers late, the production process will start late, the finished product will be completed late and the order will be delivered late. This results in a dissatisfied client, who will probably order from another business next time. In such a case the business loses the profit that could have been made from this client in future.

Contingency plans can be made to prevent late delivery of the product to clients. However, these plans usually involve considerable extra costs, which have probably not been budgeted for. For instance, instead of sending the product by rail, you may have to send it by air freight to ensure that it is delivered on time. You will then satisfy your client, but your transport costs will be much higher. If you simply cannot avoid late delivery, you may then have to incur great expense to restore the image of your business in the eyes of your clients and to retain their support.

> A small business in Jeffrey's Bay supplies leather sandals to retailers in Johannesburg and Pretoria. The production capacity of the factory is 500 pairs of sandals per day. It is now Monday. By Friday 2 500 pairs of leather sandals must be despatched by aeroplane from Port Elizabeth so that orders are delivered to retailers within the contracted time.
>
> By Monday morning the supplier of buckles has not yet delivered the 5 000 buckles needed for the sandals. This means that the factory's production activities will be delayed. The sandals can be completed up to the point where the

CHAPTER 5
The Purchasing Function

> buckles are attached, but production will then have to be halted until they arrive.
>
> The factory has only five days to complete the order and production capacity is 500 pairs per day. Because the late delivery will delay the process, workers will have to work overtime to complete the order on time. Overtime work results in higher labour costs, higher electricity costs (lights being used after hours) and other costs such as transporting employees to their homes in the evenings.

It is naturally also important that the production means are delivered to the **right place**, otherwise additional costs will be incurred getting them to the right place, and this may also cause delays in the production process.

> The best way of ensuring continuity in the business is to:
> ❑ use **good, reliable suppliers**;
> ❑ apply **effective stock control**.

We will deal with these aspects in more detail in sections 6.2 (selecting suppliers) and 6.3 (stock control).

Quality
Entrepreneurs should remember that consumers expect the product or service they buy to be of a certain quality (the 'right quality'), and that they will not be satisfied with less. The production means influence the quality of the product or service produced. It is therefore important that these production means comply with certain quality standards. See section 6.3 for an explanation of the term 'right quality'. There we will also discuss the steps to be followed to establish a quality control system in your business.

Effective stock control
The management of stock is important in any business. It is therefore essential that you exercise effective control over stock levels and purchasing quantities. Section 6.3 (stock control) provides more information on why and how you could implement an effective stock control system in your business.

Alternative suppliers
To protect the continuity of your business, you should identify various suppliers, and not just one, for the same production means. This will

ensure that another supplier can supply the production means on time if the usual supplier cannot.

Good relationships with suppliers
If suppliers have a good image of your business and good relations with its staff, they will enjoy doing business with you. In a crisis, they will go out of their way to assist you.

Good relationships with other functions in the enterprise
The various functions in the small business are interdependent. If you do not manage all these functions yourself, it is important that the purchasing manager maintains good relations with the other managers. The purchasing manager, operations manager and marketing manager must communicate effectively to avoid problems. The following example will illustrate how important this statement is.

Celia owns a factory that manufactures beachwear in light cotton, which is sold by 'surf shops' throughout South Africa. She has five representatives who travel throughout the country and take orders for her clothes. The representatives then fax these orders through to the marketing manager. The marketing manager contracts by fax with the owners of the 'surf shops' on which dates the stock will be despatched.

THE PROBLEM:
The marketing manager works completely independently of the operations manager. He therefore contracts dates with clients without ever finding out from the operations department whether they have the capacity and the time to complete the orders. The operations department can make only a certain number of dresses per day and may already have other orders to make up by this date.

To complicate matters, the purchasing manager and operations manager also do not communicate with each other, with the result that the right material for the specific orders is not available when required.

CHAPTER 5

The Purchasing Function

THE CONSEQUENCES:

These types of relationships in a business have far-reaching consequences. In the short term, orders will not be delivered on time, and often the product that is despatched is not exactly what was ordered because the right material could not be obtained. Unfortunately this is not all. In the long term, the 'surf shops' could get tired of struggling with the factory's range of clothing and order their clothes from another supplier. Eventually the demand for the factory's clothes could drop to such an extent that it is no longer profitable and the owner must close down.

WHAT SHOULD HAPPEN:

The marketing manager, operations manager and purchasing manager should meet weekly and even daily to discuss all orders and make their plans on how to deliver them. In this way they can contract realistic dates with clients and ensure that the right materials are available on time so that the correct orders are made up and sent to the client by the contracted date (see Figure 5.4).

Figure 5.4

PROBLEM		SOLUTION	
MARKETING MANAGER — plans independently		MARKETING MANAGER — Plan together	• Right production means
PURCHASING MANAGER — plans independently	POOR RELATIONS → BUSINESS CLOSES DOWN	PURCHASING MANAGER	GOOD RELATIONS
OPERATIONS MANAGER — plans independently		OPERATIONS MANAGER	• Right time • Right place

THE ENTREPRENEURSHIP SERIES
Management for Entrepreneurs

> The table below indicates a number of events or situations in a business that manufactures chocolate. How could these events/situations affect the business (the effect may be positive or negative)? Write down one consequence of each event/situation.

EVENT/SITUATION	RESULT
The business's chocolate has always been of exceptional quality. Suddenly the quality of the cocoa from the supplier drops and this causes a drop in the quality of the chocolate.	....
The business has only one supplier of cocoa.	....
The business is on good terms with the cocoa supplier.	....
The relationship between various functional managers, particularly the production manager, financial manager and purchasing manager, is not very good.	....

To ensure that the broad, long-term objectives of the business are achieved, it is necessary to formulate **short-term objectives**. These are more **specific** than broad objectives and are formulated for the **short term**. They will therefore indicate, for example, what the purchasing function should do during the following year to ensure that the broad objectives are achieved.

> As regards **quality** (a broad objective), the owner of the factory manufacturing beachwear can set the following specific objective:

CHAPTER 5
The Purchasing Function

❑ Develop a questionnaire by 31 October 20xx to be sent out by 15 November 20xx to all clients ('surf shops' that have placed one or more orders) to determine whether the new range of clothing introduced in January 20xx satisfies their quality requirements.

Note that this objective indicates exactly what must be done and by which date it must be done.

Let us look again at the example of the chocolate manufacturer. The owner formulated the broad objectives below. Now write down a short-term objective for each of the broad objectives. Indicate precisely what must be done and by which date it must be done.

BROAD OBJECTIVE	SHORT-TERM OBJECTIVE
To produce chocolate of exceptional quality	....
The business must use at least three suppliers	....
The business must have a good relationship with its cocoa suppliers	....
The relationship between the functional managers must improve so that everyone works together as a team	....

119

Finally, we can represent the relationship between the broad, long-term objectives and short-term objectives in the purchasing function as follows (see Figure 5.5). We use **quality** and **good relations with suppliers** as an example.

Figure 5.5

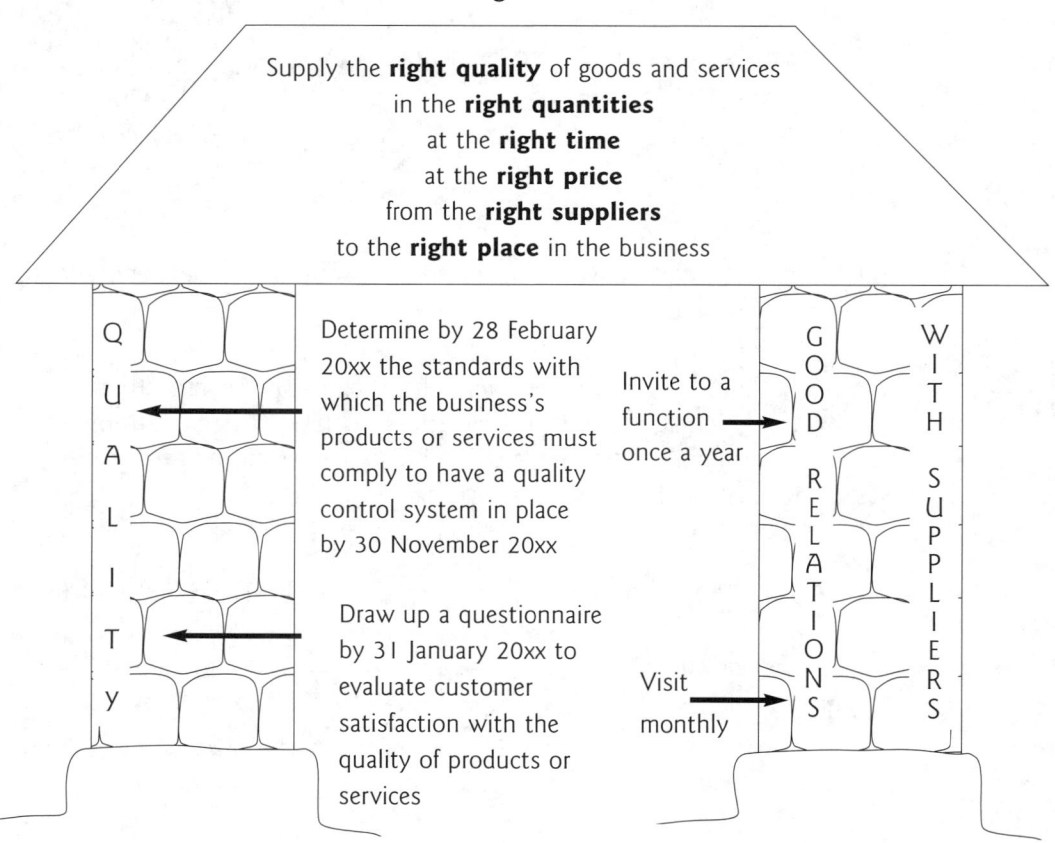

Supply the **right quality** of goods and services
in the **right quantities**
at the **right time**
at the **right price**
from the **right suppliers**
to the **right place** in the business

QUALITY

Determine by 28 February 20xx the standards with which the business's products or services must comply to have a quality control system in place by 30 November 20xx

Draw up a questionnaire by 31 January 20xx to evaluate customer satisfaction with the quality of products or services

GOOD RELATIONS

Invite to a function once a year

Visit monthly

WITH SUPPLIERS

5 ACTIVITIES OF THE PURCHASING FUNCTION

We will now look briefly at the activities that take place within the purchasing function. Remember, however, that every business is different and that the activities and the way in which they take place differ from business to business. Nonetheless, when we look at the **purchasing procedure**, it is possible to identify a number of activities that take place in the purchasing function of most businesses.

CHAPTER 5
The Purchasing Function

Figure 5.6

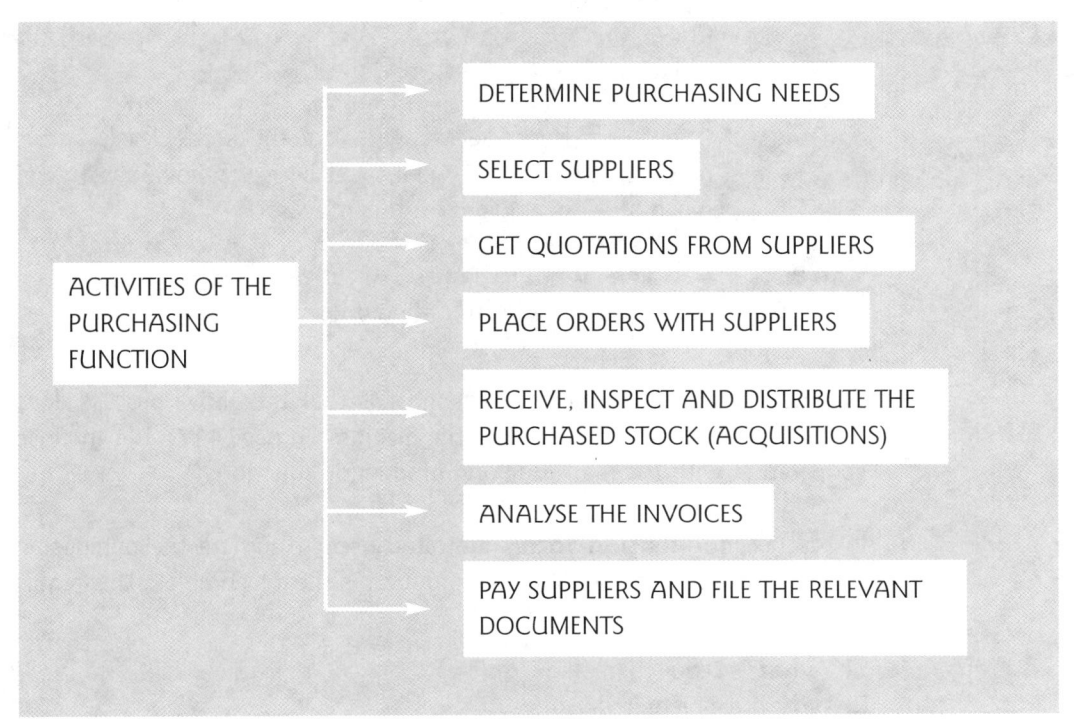

ACTIVITIES OF THE PURCHASING FUNCTION
- DETERMINE PURCHASING NEEDS
- SELECT SUPPLIERS
- GET QUOTATIONS FROM SUPPLIERS
- PLACE ORDERS WITH SUPPLIERS
- RECEIVE, INSPECT AND DISTRIBUTE THE PURCHASED STOCK (ACQUISITIONS)
- ANALYSE THE INVOICES
- PAY SUPPLIERS AND FILE THE RELEVANT DOCUMENTS

Determine purchasing needs

The activities that take place within the various functions of the business necessarily create a need for certain production means. A manufacturing business manufactures a product from certain raw materials, semi-complete products or even completed products (parts/components). These **means of production are therefore regularly required**, and this creates the need for purchasing. In the case of a retailer who simply buys final products from wholesalers or manufacturers and resells them to the consumer, the greatest purchasing need is for the final product, which must be on the shelf when the customer requires it.

In both cases, a **sales forecast** must be done at the beginning of the year, month or even week (depending on the type of business). The purpose of the forecast is to **estimate the expected sales**. The inputs of salespeople and agents, as well as of the marketing function, which analyses the needs of consumers and their purchasing patterns, are important here. We will discuss the sales forecast and other important factors in more detail in section 6.1 under the heading 'budgeting for purchasing'.

> The need for purchasing is therefore determined by:
>
> STEP 1: Forecasting expected sales
>
> STEP 2: Comparing this forecast with current stock levels and production schedules (what must be made when and how much stock is required for this process?)
>
> STEP 3: Deciding **what means of production** should be purchased and **when** it should be purchased

An important point for you to remember is that the above process does not take place in isolation (look at the diagram on page 117), but in close cooperation with the marketing and production functions.

In practice, **requisition forms** are often used to initiate the purchasing process. Those people who require production means complete this requisition, specifying exactly:

- **what** is required;
- **when** it is required;
- **what quality** is required;
- in **what quantities** it is required.

It is a good idea, as your business grows, to design and start using a requisition form. A requisition form for orders will facilitate the job of the purchasing manager/owner by establishing a basis for determining needs. A requisition form can be in written, printed or electronic format (when used on the intranet or e-mail facility of a business). A requisition form can be a useful **reference** and can even serve as **evidence** when a dispute should arise.

> The requisition form should provide for the following:
> - The **date** on which the order is placed;
> - The **name** of the person placing the order;
> - The **signature/Personal Identification Number (PIN)/ password** of the person **placing the order**;
> - The **signature/Personal Identification Number (PIN)/ password** of the person **approving the order**.

CHAPTER 5
The Purchasing Function

eg Look at the following example:

M & M FURNITURE MANUFACTURERS

REQUISITION FORM   **Nr. 8264**

SUPPLIER
Knysna Wood Suppliers
P.O. Box 368
Knysna
6570

TO:
The Head: Purchasing Department

Requisitioned by:

NAME:	Albert Smith
DEPARTMENT:	PRODUCTION
EXTENSION:	4141
DATE:	10-09-20xx
DELIVERY BEFORE OR ON:	30-09-20xx
MOTIVATION FOR PURCHASE:	Bedroom suite on order
SPECIAL INSTRUCTIONS:	Wood must be 75% dry

SIGNATURES:

Requisitioned by: *J. Smith*

Approved by: *B. Stotko*

DESCRIPTION OF GOODS	QUANTITY	UNIT PRICE	DISCOUNT	TOTAL
2,0 m x 0,25 m x 0,2 m blackwood	2	3 100,00		6 200,00

FOR OFFICE USE ONLY:

Order No: 1432   Department Code: 65

Signature: *M. Sibosa*   Date: 10-09-20xx
Buyer

SUBTOTAL	6 200,00
VAT	868,00
TOTAL	7 068,00

Select suppliers

This is very important, particularly in manufacturing businesses. As we have already explained, the whole production process can be brought to a standstill if a supplier does not deliver stock on time. If the quality of the stock is not 'right', the final product will also be substandard and therefore unacceptable.

The selection of suppliers is a very important topic that we will discuss in section 6.2 when we look at the organisation of the purchasing function.

Get quotations from suppliers

The price that you pay for your stock is very important, because it **influences the cost** of the final product. If you pay too much and the selling price is fixed (through advertising or by law or a similar provision), your profit margin will drop. You may even register a loss on that product (look again at the example on page 113). The quality of production means is also usually linked to the price paid for it. In section 6.3 we look at the link between price and quality.

In some cases, such as when the price of goods fluctuates or depends on the quantities ordered, it is advisable first to get a quotation from the supplier before you place the order. These quotations can be obtained by telephone (though this is not advisable), in writing or via e-commerce (Internet or e-mail). If you have more than one supplier for the same production means, it is advisable first to compare their quotations before you place your order.

Place orders with suppliers

Orders are usually placed through an **order form** (printed or electronic). This order form may be supplied by the supplier or by the business itself. The buyer must therefore agree with the supplier on the form to be used and the procedure to be followed.

What is important here is not whose form is used but that there **is an order form** and that a **copy of each order form is filed/saved** so that it is available later for reference if necessary. This order form is regarded as a **legal contract** that can be used as evidence in a court of law. Orders by telephone should therefore also be followed up by an official order form.

The order form must provide for the following:

- ❑ The date on which the order is placed;
- ❑ What is ordered and in what units (litres, metre lengths and so on);
- ❑ The quantity ordered;
- ❑ The quality standards required;
- ❑ Value-added tax;
- ❑ The date on which delivery must be made (if this is important for the continuity of the business's processes);
- ❑ A reference number (usually the requisition form number) and order form number (these are useful for references and coordination).

CHAPTER 5
The Purchasing Function

Look at the following example of an order form:

M & M FURNITURE MANUFACTURERS
Da Gama Avenue
Knysna
6570

Tel: 367-8430

REQUISITIONED BY: A. Smith   **ORDER FORM NO. 1432**

REQUISITION FORM NO: 8264

| SUPPLIER | Knysna Wood Suppliers
P.O. Box 368
Knysna, 6570 | Date: | 10-09-20xx |

DELIVERY DETAILS
DELIVERY DATE: 30-09-20xx
CONTACT PERSON: V. Moosa
TELEPHONE NO: 367-8431
BUILDING: M & M Furniture Manufacturers
FLOOR: Ground

PRODUCT DETAILS

Description	Unit	Quantity	Unit Price	Total
2,0 m x 0,25 m x 0,2m 75% dry blackwood	Bundles	2	3 100,00	6 200,00
			SUBTOTAL	6 200,00
			VAT	868,00
			TOTAL	7 068,00

Signature: *M. Sibosa*
Buyer

---

1. Why must the person responsible for purchasing always know what the stock levels and production schedules are?

   ....
   ....
   ....
   ....

THE ENTREPRENEURSHIP SERIES
Management for Entrepreneurs

2. Why is it useful to have a reference number on an order form?

   ....
   ....

3. Complete the following sentences by filling in the missing words:

   ❏ The price paid for stock determines the ………. of the final product.

   ❏ An order form is a ……………. that can be used as evidence in a court of law.

Receive, inspect and distribute the goods

If the place of delivery is not precisely specified on the order form, goods will usually be delivered to the reception area or to the warehouse. The person who receives the order must conduct a **superficial inspection** to determine whether the right quantity of goods was delivered and to see that the packaging is not damaged. If there is any **deviation** or problem, this must be **noted on the delivery note**. The recipient must then sign this form and keep **a copy on record**, or issue an **acknowledgement of receipt** with full particulars. Again, the procedure will depend on what has been agreed with the supplier.

What is important here is that some **proof of receipt** be kept on record. Copies of this proof are usually sent with the delivered goods to:

❏ the person who **requested** the purchase (through the requisition form);
❏ the person who must eventually **pay the account**.

The person who **finally receives the goods** must then also **inspect them thoroughly** to check whether they fulfil the specifications and quality requirements.

Look at the example of a delivery note on the following page:

CHAPTER 5
The Purchasing Function

CLIENT	DELIVERY	No. 763
M & M Furniture Manufacturers Da Gama Avenue Knysna 6570 **ORDER NO: 1432**		30-09-20xx Date **KNYSNA WOOD SUPPLIERS** Tel. 367-7624

Description	Quantity	Unit Price	Total
bundle of blackwood (75% dry)	2	3 100,00	6 200,00

Received by:

V. MOOSA

SUBTOTAL	6 200,00
VAT	868,00
TOTAL	7 068,00

If the delivered goods do not fulfil the specifications (indicated on the order form), you have the following options:

- Return the order, **cancel** it and obtain the goods from another supplier;
- Return the order and demand that the supplier **replace it within a certain period**;
- Agree with the supplier to **accept** the order **at a lower price** (if this will not have a detrimental effect on your product or service).

THE ENTREPRENEURSHIP SERIES
Management for Entrepreneurs

> Refusal to accept orders is a sensitive issue that in some cases may even result in court cases. The golden rule here is therefore: **handle the matter diplomatically and with sensitivity!**

Analyse the invoices

Invoices can be received via the post or e-commerce (Internet/e-mail). It is very important that you analyse every invoice you receive from a supplier. Also **compare** the invoice with:

❏ the **order form** (this process is facilitated if you ensure that every order form is numbered and you use this number as a reference number for the transaction);
❏ the **quotation** (if the supplier provided a written or electronic quotation).

Make sure that the quantities, price and specifications on the invoice correspond with the order and quotation and that the discounts agreed upon were also taken into account. Discounts are also sometimes offered if the supplier is paid within a specific period. Note such provisions and take advantage of these discounts if your cash flow permits. These can eventually make a considerable difference to your profit.

Look at the following example of an invoice:

CLIENT	TAX INVOICE	No. 1733
M & M Furniture Manufacturers Da Gama Avenue Knysna 6570 **ORDER NO: 1432**		Date: 30-09-20xx **KNYSNA WOOD SUPPLIERS** P.O. Box 368 Knysna 6570

Date	Description	Unit Price	Total
30-09-20xx	2 bundles blackwood (2,0 x 0,25 x 0,2 m)	3 100,00	6 200,00
	& VAT		868,00
	Delivery note no. 763		7 068,00

SIGNATURE: _____

CHAPTER 5
The Purchasing Function

Pay suppliers and file the relevant documents

If your business has grown to the extent that a specific person (a financial manager, for example) is responsible for the finances, this person will take over this task. In such a case it is a good idea to design and use a **payment request**. On this form the purchasing officer or purchasing manager requests and authorises the financial manager (with a signature or PIN/password) to pay the invoice. The financial manager can then assume that all the documentation has been checked and is correct, and can proceed with the payment. This can be done by cheque or electronic payment into suppliers' banking accounts.

If you are personally responsible for both purchasing and finances, you should write your cheque number or electronic payment reference and date on the invoice and file it together with all the documentation until you receive your cheque back from the bank or a receipt from the supplier. Now attach all other documentation and file it together with the invoice for later reference. In Chapter 7 we look at the implementation of a filing or information system that enables you easily to trace a specific transaction when you require information about it.

What documentation are you currently using for purchasing? Also indicate the purpose of this documentation in your business.

DOCUMENT	PURPOSE

Do the documents that you mentioned above meet the requirements discussed in this chapter? If not, adapt them or design a new set of documents that you can use to formalise your purchasing activities and ensure that you have effective records of all your transactions.

6 MANAGEMENT OF THE PURCHASING FUNCTION

In Chapter 1 we looked at the four main functions of general management: **planning, organising, leadership and control**. These functions are also performed in the purchasing department. Because leadership is a fairly broad concept, we will not look at this any further. However, it is important that we briefly discuss the other three functions.

Figure 5.7

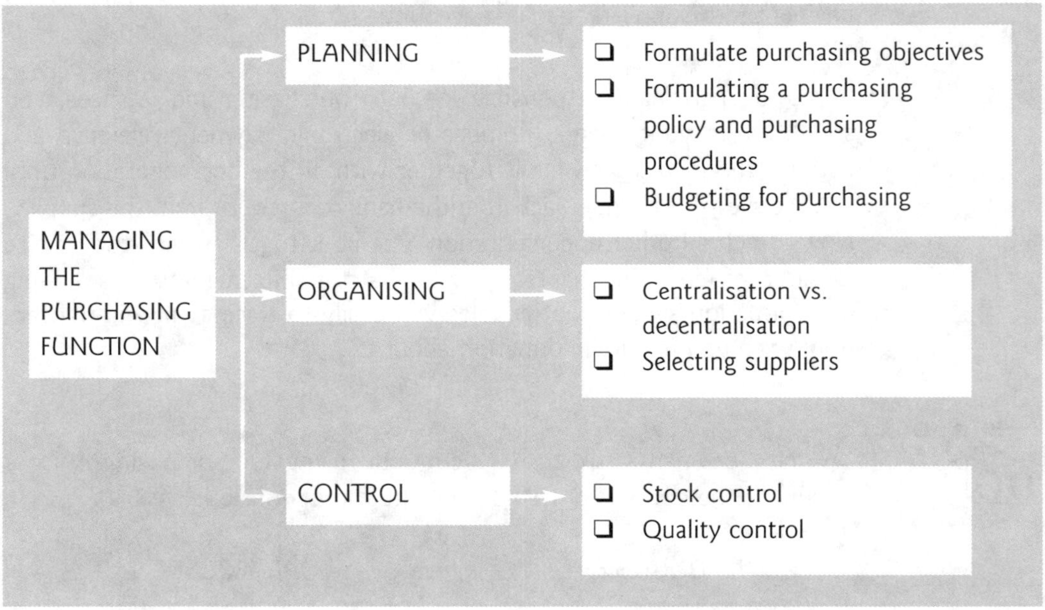

```
                    ┌─ PLANNING ──→  ❑ Formulate purchasing objectives
                    │                 ❑ Formulating a purchasing
                    │                   policy and purchasing
                    │                   procedures
                    │                 ❑ Budgeting for purchasing
MANAGING            │
THE          ───────┼─ ORGANISING ─→ ❑ Centralisation vs.
PURCHASING          │                   decentralisation
FUNCTION            │                 ❑ Selecting suppliers
                    │
                    └─ CONTROL ────→ ❑ Stock control
                                      ❑ Quality control
```

6.1 Planning for purchasing

Formulate purchasing objectives
Planning for purchasing starts with the formulation of broad, long-term objectives and short-term objectives. This process was discussed in section 4.

Formulating a purchasing policy and purchasing procedures
If your business is still so small that you take responsibility for all the functions yourself, this aspect will not yet be important to you. However, as soon as you start delegating functions and responsibilities in the business to other people, a purchasing policy and purchasing procedures will become essential.

CHAPTER 5
The Purchasing Function

The **purchasing policy** determines the **guidelines** according to which suppliers are identified and selected, and the **basic principles** according to which they are treated.

> **NB**
>
> The purchasing policy sets guidelines on aspects such as the following:
>
> ❑ Must we use only local suppliers, or can foreign suppliers also be approached?
> ❑ Will we use only one supplier per production means, or must we use various suppliers per product?
> ❑ Will we buy direct from the manufacturer, or must we use intermediaries?
> ❑ May we accept gifts and benefits from suppliers?
> ❑ May we conclude reciprocal agreements with suppliers? For instance, may I buy all my rubber from Company A on condition that this company buys all its tyres from me?

As the name indicates, **purchasing procedures** set out the procedures to be followed in the purchasing process. It stipulates **what** must be done, **by whom** it must be done and **how** it must be done.

A purchasing policy and clear purchasing procedures will save much frustration and many future problems, especially when your business has many different branches and various people who do the purchasing. This is a simple way of ensuring that purchasing takes place according to set guidelines and procedures and that confusion is avoided.

Budgeting for purchasing
We all know that no activity can take place without funds. You should therefore budget carefully for purchasing. In Chapter 2 we mentioned that the budget is an extremely important aid in the planning of the business's capital needs of your business. The **budget of the purchasing function is part of the annual budget**. You should therefore look carefully at the financial needs of the purchasing function for the next financial period and budget for these. By budgeting for your future needs, you will ensure that funds are available when they are required.

A purchasing budget usually starts with a **forecast of expected sales** for the next financial period. If you alone are responsible for the finances, purchasing, operations and marketing of your business, this should not be a complicated task. However, when more people are involved, it is very important that you get the people responsible for **finances, marketing, operations** and **purchasing** together to do a **realistic needs analysis** before each draws up his or her own functional budget.

❑ The marketing staff must first indicate what they expect their sales to be.
❑ The operations staff then work out what they require for production or for providing services.
❑ The purchasing staff must then determine their purchasing needs according to the operations staff's estimate of needs.

On the basis of these figures, the purchasing staff must now communicate with suppliers and establish **prices** for the next financial period. A **purchasing budget** is then drawn up on the basis of all relevant and available information. This purchasing budget is given to the financial manager, who will include it in the annual budget of the business.

> In some businesses (such as those that have functioned in a certain industry for a long time and have an established client base), it is fairly easy to draw up a sales forecast. In others, such as local grocery stores, it is much more difficult. However, in such cases it is possible to design an effective records system with a computer package or coding system. Such a system will help you to establish, over a period of a few months, more or less how much of each product is sold every month. Using this information, you can then identify certain trends and purchasing patterns and make a more realistic sales forecast.

Talk to an expert in the field of purchasing to determine which computer packages are available and which will best suit the needs of your business.

> 1. Draw up a list of people in your business that you would involve in budgeting for purchasing. Indicate the position of each within the business and what their roles would be in drawing up the budget.

CHAPTER 5

The Purchasing Function

PERSON'S NAME	POSITION IN BUSINESS	ROLE IN COMPILING PURCHASING BUDGET
....	....	....
....	....	....
....	....	....
....	....	....
....	....	....
....	....	....
....	....	....
....	....	....

2. List three computer packages that could be suitable for planning the purchasing function in your business.

   ....
   ....
   ....

6.2 Organising the purchasing function

Centralisation vs. decentralisation

In new small businesses, the activities are usually all carried out in one place. As your business grows, however, you may find that you open **various branches** or, later, even various **regional offices**. It is therefore important to note the difference between centralised and decentralised purchasing.

In a small business, purchasing is naturally centralised. As the **business grows**, you may consider **decentralising** your purchasing function. For instance, it may be impractical to have to send all requisitions to head office and then to despatch all the purchased stock to the branches or regional offices again. In many businesses, time is crucial and decentralised purchasing can make the business more effective.

In practice, **decentralisation** simply means that every branch and/or region has a person responsible for purchasing. This person then deals with the purchasing activities of that particular branch and/or region.

If you decide to decentralise your purchasing activities, it is important to ensure that your business first has an established **purchasing policy** and **purchasing procedures**. This will ensure that buyers know what they may and may not do and also how they should set about their jobs. Use standard procedures and forms to prevent confusion and to promote coordination.

Businesses with **centralised purchasing departments** often buy **in bulk**. This means that they can negotiate **quantity discounts** with suppliers. Centralisation of the purchasing function also **promotes good relations with suppliers** because the supplier works with a limited number of buyers.

A **disadvantage of centralisation** is that it can become an **extensive process**. Particularly where the production process in branches or regions is dependent on receiving certain means of production on time, it may be more beneficial rather to decentralise the purchasing activities. In cases where raw material needs or standards differ from region to region, decentralisation is also a good option.

Selecting suppliers
The first step in selecting suppliers is to **identify** potential suppliers. Determine which suppliers offer the production means that you require, and then set **criteria** according to which you measure them so that you can eventually **select** those suppliers that best fulfil your needs.

Selecting suppliers involves four steps:

1. IDENTIFY POTENTIAL SUPPLIERS

2. SET CRITERIA FOR EVALUATING SUPPLIERS

3. EVALUATE AND SELECT SUPPLIERS

4. MONITOR SUPPLIERS

CHAPTER 5

The Purchasing Function

> **There are various ways of identifying potential suppliers.**
> Below are a few suggestions:
>
> ❑ Consult **other businesses** with the same needs.
> ❑ Look in **specialist periodicals** (trade magazines), such as an iron and steel industries periodical if you require a supplier in this industry.
> ❑ Look in the **Yellow Pages**.
> ❑ Attend **shows** where potential suppliers exhibit their products.
> ❑ Contact your local **chamber of business** to find out who supplies the production means that you require.
> ❑ Look on the Internet.

Once you have identified potential suppliers, set **criteria** for their evaluation and eventual selection. Aspects you could consider include:

❑ The **geographic location** of a supplier will be important in terms of transport costs and delivery time.
❑ The **reputation** of the supplier will indicate whether the supplier is reliable in terms of punctuality and service.
❑ The **quality, price and features** of the supplier's products will indicate whether the product is suitable for your needs.

The last step in selecting your suppliers is to **monitor** them. It is extremely important once suppliers have been used for the first time to evaluate them thoroughly to determine whether they kept to the terms of your agreement, whether their goods were of the right quality and whether they were delivered at the correct time to the correct place. Apart from this initial evaluation, all your suppliers should be monitored constantly to identify problems, solve them or possibly change suppliers.

> 1. Think about all the factors involved in providing your specific product or service and the success of your business, and identify your expectations of suppliers. From this you can formulate criteria according to which you will evaluate potential suppliers for your small business and write them down in the space provided.

THE ENTREPRENEURSHIP SERIES
Management for Entrepreneurs

My criteria for suppliers are the following:

....
....
....
....
....
....

2. Think about the characteristics and future growth potential of your business. Would it be beneficial to decentralise your purchasing activities in future, or would it be better to remain centralised? Motivate your answer by referring to the advantages and disadvantages of your choice.

Later, my business would benefit from:
DECENTRALISATION   YES   NO
The reasons for my choice are as follows:

....
....
....
....
....
....
....
....

6.3 Controlling purchasing

Stock control

Stock is very important in any business, simply because:

CHAPTER 5

The Purchasing Function

❑ **production** and the provision of services cannot continue without stock;
❑ without stock, the **needs of clients** will not be satisfied;
❑ keeping stock **is costly**.

As regards costs, we think of the cost of orders and inspections, as well as actual stocking-keeping (or inventory) costs. These include rental and electrification of the warehouse, insurance and the salaries of warehouse staff. An additional cost is the cost of 'running out of stock'. Here we mean the costs that arise from keeping insufficient stock, which hampers the production or marketing process. We have looked at examples in this regard earlier. Refer to section 4.

The costs associated with stock therefore include:

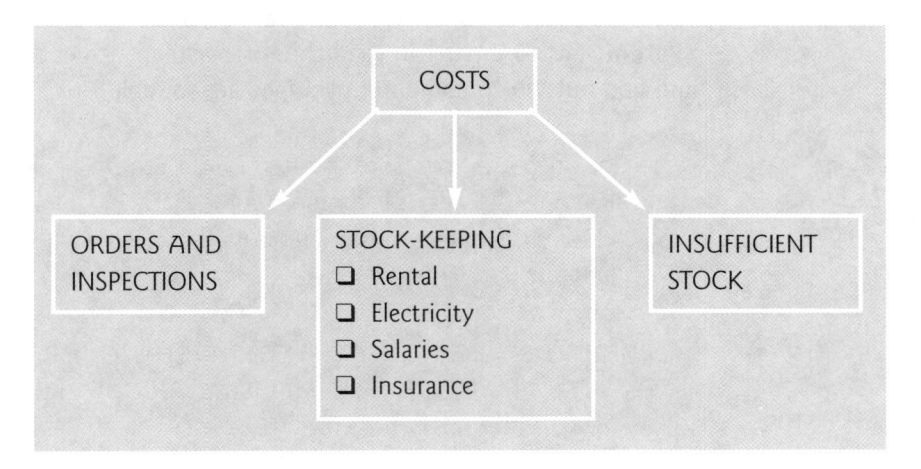

```
                         COSTS
          ↙                ↓                ↘
  ORDERS AND        STOCK-KEEPING       INSUFFICIENT
  INSPECTIONS       ❑ Rental            STOCK
                    ❑ Electricity
                    ❑ Salaries
                    ❑ Insurance
```

From the above you can see that stock must be properly managed. A business should be neither overstocked nor understocked. **Determine optimum stock levels** for your business. Weigh up the costs of keeping stock versus the costs of running out of stock, and determine from this how much 'safety stock' you should keep to provide for unforeseen circumstances.

Various formulas and methods are used to calculate optimum stock levels and the size of the safety stock. However, certain methods are suitable for certain types of businesses and not always for others.

One example is the **scanning system used by certain large chain stores**.

THE ENTREPRENEURSHIP SERIES

Management for Entrepreneurs

> When a product is scanned at the paypoint, the scanner registers both the product as well as the price, and prints these details on the client's till slip. The item is simultaneously removed from the stock register. Management is therefore always aware of the stock levels of every product. It is even possible to activate orders automatically by computer when the stock levels of a specific product fall below a certain level.

Naturally such a sophisticated system is fairly expensive, and not every small business will be able to afford it. **Your aim as a small business entrepreneur is to achieve the same effectiveness with a simpler system.** Talk to experts in the field of stock management in your industry and find out which computer packages are suitable.

1. Consider the costs associated with stock in your business, including the cost of 'running out' of stock. Complete the table below. Write down the amount associated with each of the components below.

ORDERING COSTS	INSPECTION COSTS	STOCK-KEEPING COSTS	COST OF RUNNING OUT OF STOCK

2. Once you have listed all these costs, ask an expert in the field of purchasing and computer packages to determine the optimum

CHAPTER 5

The Purchasing Function

stock levels for your business. Ask this person how much safety stock you should keep. Then complete the table below. If your stock consists of a variety of production means, draw up a list of how much of each item should be kept in stock and in the safety stock.

OPTIMUM STOCK LEVELS FOR	SAFETY STOCK LEVELS FOR
....	....
....	....
....	....
....	....
....	....
....	....
....	....
....	....

Quality control

The marketing manager (and/or owner) of a business is in constant contact with clients. This person specifies the quality standards with which each product or service must comply.

Figure 5.8

CLIENTS ↔ MARKETING MANAGER/OWNER ↔ OPERATIONS DEPARTMENT

QUALITY STANDARDS

In his/her calculations the marketing manager/owner must look thoroughly at:
- the **costs of various levels of quality**;
- the **price that the consumer is prepared to pay** for the product or service.

The 'right quality' is therefore the highest-quality product/service that can be supplied at the price that the client is prepared to pay. With regard to purchasing, the **'right quality'** is therefore **not necessarily the highest quality**, but that which fulfils the specifications of the operations department. A higher quality should be bought only if it does not result in higher costs, and if it will not affect availability of the product/service. In this context the 'right quality' is defined as follows:

> The **'right quality'** is the minimum acceptable quality with which production means must comply to ensure that the final product/service is acceptable to consumers.

Because quality is so important, it is advisable to implement a **quality control system** to ensure that the production means meet the quality standards. A quality control system consists of the following components:

QUALITY CONTROL SYSTEM

1. SET STANDARDS OF QUALITY
2. COMPARE THE QUALITY OF THE PRODUCTION MEANS WITH THE SET STANDARD
3. REPORT DEVIATIONS
4. TAKE CORRECTIVE ACTION

QUALITY CONTROL SYSTEM

❏ **SET STANDARDS OF QUALITY**
Consult the operations manager and write down his/her minimum standards for a specific means of production. For instance, the production manager of a stock feed supplier might specify that a minimum of B-grade maize should be used in their chicken feed.

CHAPTER 5
The Purchasing Function

- **COMPARE THE QUALITY OF THE PRODUCTION MEANS WITH THE SET STANDARD**
  Inspect the delivered means of production and ensure that it complies with standards. For instance, on delivery of the order the purchasing manager in the stock feed business notes that the maize is C grade.

- **REPORT DEVIATIONS**
  The purchasing manager informs the operations manager of the deviation and its extent (for instance, in our example there is a one-grade difference).

- **TAKE CORRECTIVE ACTION**
  The maize order is returned and the supplier undertakes to replace the order with B-grade maize within 24 hours.

HERE IT IS IMPORTANT to note that **various types of corrective action** can be taken, depending on the business and its products (see also section 5). If the quality of the delivered production means is lower than the standard but the product will not be affected by it, you may agree to accept the order at a reduced price.

THE GOLDEN RULE is therefore first to determine the effect of the deviation on the final product, and then to make a decision accordingly.

The fact that the supplier delivered the incorrect quality without negotiating this with you can affect future trade relations. The issue should therefore be cleared up immediately and the supplier should undertake not to make the same mistake in future. If this happens repeatedly, you should find another supplier.

Talk to your clients and your marketing and operations staff and then determine standards with which your final product/service and production means should comply to be of the 'right quality'.

THE ENTREPRENEURSHIP SERIES

Management for Entrepreneurs

> MY PRODUCT/SERVICE MUST COMPLY WITH THE FOLLOWING STANDARDS TO BE OF THE 'RIGHT QUALITY':
>
> ....
>
> ....
>
> ....
>
> ....
>
> ....
>
> THE PRODUCTION MEANS PURCHASED MUST MEET THE FOLLOWING STANDARDS TO ENABLE ME TO DELIVER A PRODUCT OF THE 'RIGHT QUALITY' TO CLIENTS.

PRODUCTION MEANS REQUIRED TO PRODUCE MY PRODUCT/SERVICE	STANDARDS THAT THESE PRODUCTION MEANS MUST MEET
....	....
....	....
....	....
....	....
....	....
....	....

SUMMARY

In this chapter we investigated the role, importance and functioning of the purchasing function in the small business. We looked specifically at the objectives of the purchasing function, its activities and its management.

Use the practical tips and examples in the chapter when planning and managing the purchasing activities in your small business.

CHAPTER 5
The Purchasing Function

SELF-EVALUATION

1. Briefly explain the role and importance of the purchasing function in your small business.

   ....
   ....
   ....

2. Write down three broad, long-term objectives and three short-term objectives for the purchasing function in your enterprise.

   ....
   ....
   ....
   ....
   ....
   ....

3. Briefly write down what purchasing activities you or the purchasing manager carries out in your business.

   ....
   ....
   ....
   ....
   ....
   ....

4. Formulate a purchasing policy for your small business.

   ....
   ....
   ....
   ....
   ....

5. Formulate a set of procedures according to which you would organise the purchasing activities in your business.

   ....
   ....

THE ENTREPRENEURSHIP SERIES
Management for Entrepreneurs

....
....
....

6. Will a centralised or a decentralised purchasing system be suitable for your business in the future? Motivate your choice by referring to the advantages of the particular system. What are the disadvantages of the system you have chosen for your business?

   TYPE OF SYSTEM: ....

ADVANTAGES	DISADVANTAGES
....	....
....	....
....	....
....	....
....	....
....	....
....	....

7. List five ways to identify suppliers for your business.

   1. .... 2. ....
   3. .... 4. ....
   5. ....

8. List the various criteria according to which you would evaluate suppliers for your business.

   ....
   ....
   ....
   ....
   ....

CHAPTER 5

The Purchasing Function

9. Explain the costs associated with stock in your business.

   ....
   ....
   ....
   ....
   ....

10. List three computer packages or other systems that you could use to control stock in your business.

    ....
    ....
    ....

11. How would you apply quality control in the purchasing function of your business? Refer specifically to the steps you would follow, the standards with which your product/service and production means must comply and the various corrective steps that you could take.

QUALITY CONTROL

....
....
....
....
....
....

CORRECTIVE STEPS

....
....
....
....
....
....

REFERENCES

Bivins, B.M. 1994. *Operating a Really Small Business: An Owner's Guide.* Menlo Park, California: Crisp.

Cronje, G.J. de J., Neuland, E.W., Hugo, W.M.J. & Van Reenen, M.J. 1994. *Inleiding tot die Bestuurswese.* 3rd edition. Pretoria: Southern.

Du Plessis, P.G. 1996. *Toegepaste Ondernemingsbestuur: 'n Inleidende Oorsig.* Pretoria: Kagiso.

Hugo, W.M.J., Van Rooyen, D.C. & Badenhorst, J.A. 1997. *Aankope en Materiaalbestuur.* 3rd edition. Pretoria: Van Schaik.

Le Roux *et al.* 1999. *Business Management: A Practical and Interactive Approach.* 2nd edition. Sandton: Heinemann.

Marx, S., Van Rooyen, D.C., Bosch, J.K. & Reynders (eds). 1998. *Ondernemingsbestuur.* 2nd edition. Pretoria: Van Schaik.

Siropolis, N. 1994. *Small Business Management: A Guide to Entrepreneurship.* 5th edition. Boston: Houghton Mifflin.

Wright, C. 1995. *Small Business Management in South Africa.* 6th edition. Sandton: Struik.

6 THE HUMAN RESOURCE FUNCTION

1 LEARNING OBJECTIVES (OUTCOMES)

After you have studied this chapter, you should be able to:

- draw up a job description for a post;
- describe the process for employing staff;
- compile an induction programme;
- draw up the framework for a training programme;
- explain the remuneration of employees.

2 INTRODUCTION

Large organisations usually have a separate human resources department to deal with staff matters. In your own business, however, you will probably have to deal with the human resource function yourself. Appointing and retaining the right staff is extremely important, because every person in a small business has a considerable effect on the general work performance and productivity of the business.

The growth and development of the business depend not only on the owner, but also on the other employees. The employees you choose must enjoy their work and be loyal towards the business. Think of the service that you get every time you go to a bank or a supermarket. You would not support such a place unless you were made to feel welcome there and were treated in a friendly manner. To ensure that your business also delivers friendly service, you should therefore appoint the right people and manage them in such a way that they are productive and happy in their work.

Before you appoint people, you must first plan. You must know what type of people and how many of them you need to be able to run your business successfully. You will therefore have to do a **job analysis**. During this process you gather important data on the job. From this job analysis you can then compile:

- a **job description**;
- a **job specification**.

In this chapter we will look in more detail at human resource planning, motivation, training and development, remuneration and labour relations.

3 JOB DESCRIPTION

> A **job description** describes the duties, relationships of authority and responsibilities of a person in the work situation.

When compiling a job description, first draw up a **list of all the tasks** that must be performed in the business. (Ask the people who work there or watch what they do. If you have not employed anyone yet, work through all that they will have to do step by step.) Then **group** together the tasks that can logically be done by one person, such as all the tasks to do with money, income and expenditure. This combination of tasks can then become one person's job. We call this description of duties a job description (see Figure 6.1 in section 4).

To help you, we will first look at an example.

> Assume you own a clothes shop and want to expand. You decide to add a shoe department. Someone will have to be in charge of the work in the shoe department, and you will therefore have to draw up a job description for this post.
>
> **You start by drawing up a list of all the tasks that must be done. Below are a few of them:**
> 1. Conduct market research – see what sizes, types and quantities of shoes must be purchased.
> 2. Purchase stocks.

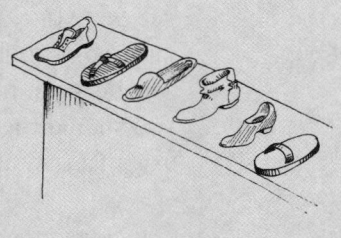

CHAPTER 6
The Human Resource Function

3. Exhibit your shoes.
4. Maintain stocks at optimum levels.
5. Sell the shoes.
6. Keep a record of accounts.
7. Keep the books up to date.
8. Calculate ordering and stock quantities.
9. Market the department.
10. Coordinate continually with the owner.

Now group together the tasks that can be done by one person.
Person 1:   Tasks 1, 2, 4, 9, 10.   For instance, a head of department.
Person 2:   Tasks 3, 5.   For instance, a salesperson.
Person 3:   Tasks 6, 7, 8.   For instance, an accounting clerk.

You could therefore appoint three people, but if the new department is still too small to warrant this, you could link some of the jobs so that only two people need be appointed. You may also use the accounting clerk from the clothes shop to take charge of the accounts of the shoe department on a temporary basis. These duties should then be added to the person's job description.

You can therefore see that, to start with, you will definitely need a head of department and a salesperson.

You can now draw up the job descriptions for these people. These should be drawn up so that the work poses a **challenge** and keeps the employee busy **the whole day through**. If there is not enough work, you may decide to give the employee two or even more different types of work.

Below is an abbreviated example of a job description that can be used in a small business. Adapt it where necessary. Also look at Figure 6.1 (in section 4) for more information that you can add.

Job title: Secretary
Section: Administration
Summary of work: Secretarial duties for the department.
                       Take charge of administrative matters.
                       Calculations for budget and remuneration
                       purposes.

THE ENTREPRENEURSHIP SERIES
Management for Entrepreneurs

Duties:	Most regular duties (at least 70% of the day): Typing all reports Keeping manager's or entrepreneur's diary Calculating office budget Less regular duties (less than 30% of the day): Filing documents Designing forms
Equipment:	Computer with word processing package Copying machine
Forms and reports used:	Budget, paysheet forms, staff evaluation forms, petty cash payments
Supervisor:	Piet Mahale (head of department)

Now draw up a **job description** for the head of the shoe department in our example above, or for a post in your own business. Look at the duties in the example. You may add to them if you wish.

....
....
....
....
....

4 JOB SPECIFICATION

You now know that the work involves those jobs that the person must be able to do. The next step is to determine **what background the person needs** to be able to do the job. You must therefore compile a **job specification**.

A **job specification** is a description of everything that a person needs to be able to do the work. Examples of this are qualifications, skills, experience, knowledge of the work and physical ability.

150

CHAPTER 6
The Human Resource Function

Look at Figure 6.1. It indicates the difference between the job description and the job specification.

Figure 6.1

JOB ANALYSIS
This is the process whereby important information about a job is collected.

JOB DESCRIPTION	JOB SPECIFICATION
This is a statement embracing the following items:	This states what qualifications an applicant needs to hold in order to be able to do the work, namely:
Job title	Training
Location	Experience
Summary of work	Education
Duties	Powers of judgement
Machinery and tools	Physical strength
Materials	Physical skills
Supervision	Responsibility
Working conditions	Communication skills
Dangers related to the job	
(It is about the job)	(It is about the person)

Source: Le Roux, E.E. *et al.*, 1999:142

THE ENTREPRENEURSHIP SERIES

Management for Entrepreneurs

---

eg

Let us take another look at the head of department in our example. The person must be able to:

❏ conduct market research;
❏ take charge of purchasing;
❏ determine optimum stock levels;

and must have:
❏ some knowledge of marketing;
❏ management skills;

What does the person therefore need to be able to do the work? You can, for instance, say that the person needs the following:

❏ **Training** – a post-school qualification in marketing, such as a diploma;
❏ **Experience** in the clothing industry;
❏ **Good judgement**, to determine which styles are popular at any particular time;
❏ **Management skills**, because the salesperson will probably work as a subordinate to the head of the department. If the business expands, there will be more subordinates;
❏ **Responsibility** to run a department;
❏ **Communication skills**, particularly when dealing with suppliers.

DO

Draw up a **job specification** for the salesperson in the shoe shop, following the example above.

....
....
....

NB

The job description and job specification are important aids for the owner of a small business. They are used for:

❏ appointing new employees (recruitment and selection);
❏ control purposes;
❏ merit assessments;
❏ promotions;
❏ the identification of training needs;
❏ the establishment of salary scales.

CHAPTER 6

The Human Resource Function

Keep a job description and job specification for every type of job in your business. These will definitely help you with all of the above tasks.

> How would you use a job description in your business?
> ....
> ....

HUMAN RESOURCE PLANNING

Now that you know what type of employees you need and how many, you can start to look for them and invite them to apply for the posts. If you already have a few employees who are suitable for the vacant posts, you may think of promoting them. However, if this is not possible, you must look for suitable employees outside the business. You therefore need to recruit employees.

You must employ only the **right number** and the **right type of employees**. Be careful not to appoint too many people: a **surplus** of staff always creates problems and may lead to retrenchments, resignations, early retirements and a division of work. A **shortage** need not always be overcome only by appointing new staff; other arrangements can also be made, such as having staff work overtime, training present staff and subcontracting outside staff. However, such situations may also lead to your staff being overworked and to a decrease in productivity. Staff members may even resign.

> What **temporary** measures can you take if your business has too few staff to do the work?
> ....
> ....

Human resource planning involves the following:

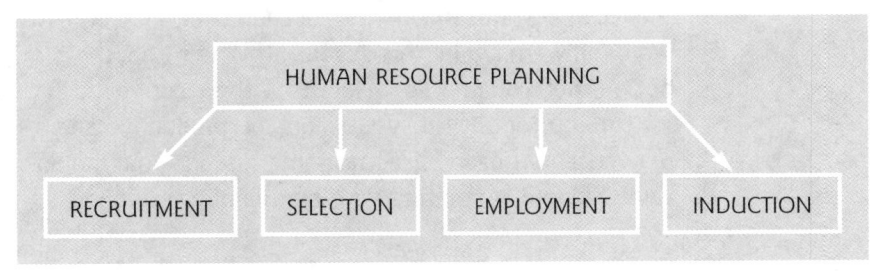

```
                    HUMAN RESOURCE PLANNING
                              |
        ┌─────────────┬───────┴───────┬─────────────┐
   RECRUITMENT    SELECTION       EMPLOYMENT     INDUCTION
```

THE ENTREPRENEURSHIP SERIES

Management for Entrepreneurs

5.1 Recruitment

> **Recruitment** involves all the activities carried out in searching for and inviting potential employees and suitable people to apply for the posts available in a business. Recruitment is involved when, for instance, an advertisement is placed in a newspaper for a secretary.

First get all the relevant details on the vacant post from the job description and job specification. You can then evaluate potential employees against these to see whether they are suitable for the job. Use this information as the criterion for assessing the candidate.

Where do you start with the recruitment process?

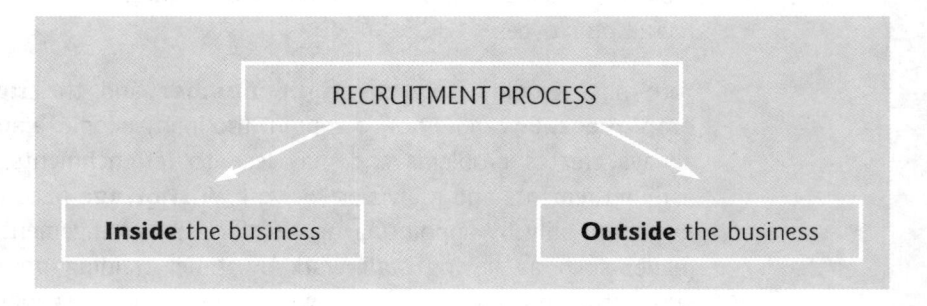

```
                    RECRUITMENT PROCESS
                    ↙              ↘
            Inside the business      Outside the business
```

Within the business you should keep **records of employees' skills**. For instance, you should keep on file details of employees' experience and qualifications, training and the courses they have attended. When a vacant post arises, you can then compare the job specification with the records to identify a suitable candidate. Open a personal file for each of your employees and keep it in a cabinet in your office.

You can also use **references**. This method is used partly within and partly outside the business. For instance, current employees may recommend their families and friends for vacant posts. However, we should sound a word of warning in this regard. This may be the simplest recruitment option, but you should ensure that the recommended people are suitable for the job, or they may later not be productive and such appointments may cost you dearly. For the same reason, you should also be extremely careful before appointing your own family and friends.

CHAPTER 6
The Human Resource Function

You should deal with a person recommended in this way in the same way as all other applicants.

Outside the business you can advertise and use the following sources:
- **Training institutions**, such as schools, technikons and universities;
- **Recruitment agencies** who recruit on behalf of the business;
- **Professional bodies** such as the South African Institute of Chartered Accountants;
- **Advertisements** in newspapers, periodicals and other media;
- Applicants at **employment agencies**.

If you are looking for a specific type of employee, you may advertise specifically. Lower-level posts, secretaries, artisans, sales staff and similar posts can be advertised in the **local newspaper**.

Some specialist periodicals can also be used. For instance, if you are looking for a marketing person, advertise in a marketing periodical. You can also advertise in the **newsletters of professional organisations**. Human resource professionals and accountants, for instance, have associations through which you can advertise.

When middle- and higher-level posts are advertised, you may wish to advertise more widely, such as in the **Sunday newspapers** or **national periodicals**. Advertisements in the latter will, of course, cost much more than those in local newspapers.

> To **compile an advertisement**, include the following information:
> - Job title;
> - Salary;
> - Important features of the work;
> - Requirements of the successful applicant;
> - Fringe benefits;
> - Application procedures;
> - The person in charge of applications;
> - A brief description of the business.
>
> Also look at current advertisements to give you more ideas.

THE ENTREPRENEURSHIP SERIES
Management for Entrepreneurs

Included below is an example of an advertisement.

Figure 6.2

Regional Managers

**Western Cape • George • Port Elizabeth • East London
• Louis Trichardt or Pietersburg • Upington
• Ermelo or Waterval-Boven • Welkom**

Keymatrix, a leader in the specialised lending industry, seeks dynamic achievers in middle-management positions in the above areas.

Your brief will be to: • manage and control 8 offices • effectively manage personnel • handle cash and budget control • initiate successful marketing programmes • oversee general administration • supply relevant statistics • control Information Technology.

Minimum requirements include: • Std 10 • sound management experience.

Important personal criteria must reflect: • strong business and client orientation • a decisive and action-orientated approach • the ability to set and achieve goals • the capability of developing and empowering team members • the ability to identify and solve problems • well-developed planning and organising skills • the foresight and initiative to continually maintain and upgrade systems • a willingness to travel.

Please forward a detailed CV and covering letter in strictest confidence to Leezelle Koen, HR: Recruitment & Selection on fax (021) 880-1863 or email: leezelle@keymatrix.com. Closing date: 30 March 2000. Please state clearly the area for which you are applying.

Write an advertisement for one of the vacant posts in your business.

....
....
....
....

CHAPTER 6
The Human Resource Function

☞

....
....
....
....
....
....
....
....
....
....
....
....
....
....
....
....
....

When recruiting, all positive and negative aspects of the job must be pointed out to the potential applicants. Possible candidates are screened here already and invited to apply. They may also be invited to look around the business to get more ideas of the working conditions.

Assume you need the following types of employees in your business. How would you set about recruiting them?

1. Engineer ....
2. Boilermaker..
3. Salesperson ....

5.2 Selection

Once potential employees have applied or indicated that they are interested in the posts, the selection process starts.

Selection is the process in which the most suitable person for a vacant post is chosen from among the applicants for the post.

You can use the following **steps** to help you in the **selection process**:

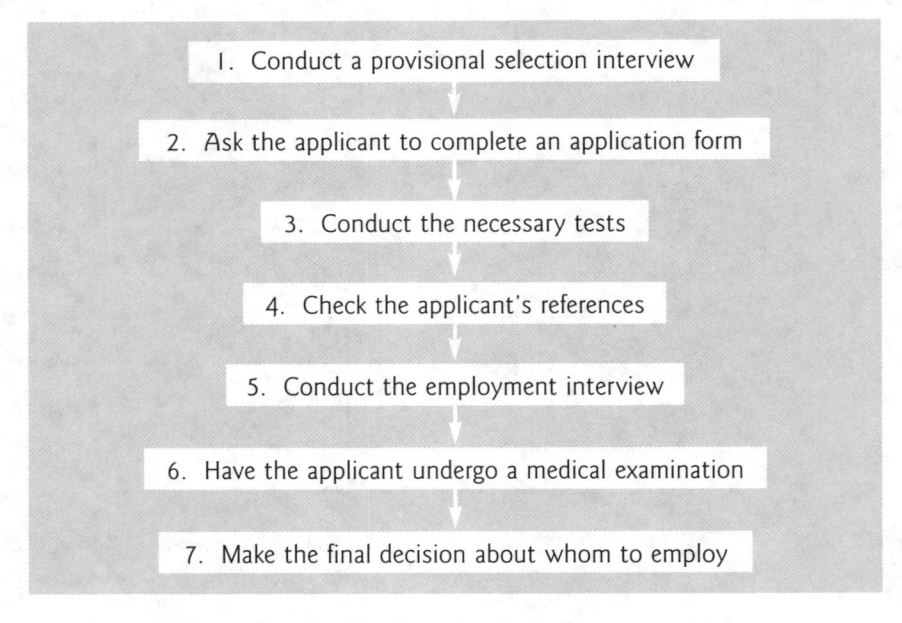

1. Conduct a provisional selection interview
2. Ask the applicant to complete an application form
3. Conduct the necessary tests
4. Check the applicant's references
5. Conduct the employment interview
6. Have the applicant undergo a medical examination
7. Make the final decision about whom to employ

Conduct a provisional selection interview
Determine whether the applicant's qualifications and interests are suitable for the requirements of the post. If so, continue with the process.

Ask the applicant to complete an application form
Evaluate the information on the form. Compare the information with the specifications. Try to decide now whether the applicant is suitable. (If you do not have an application form, have a look at the forms that other businesses use and design your own.)

Conduct the necessary tests
The type of work will determine the tests that need to be done. Applicants are tested to obtain extra information on, for instance, their intelligence, skills (such as typing speed) and personality (are they able to work with people or not. Is the applicant withdrawn, shy or friendly?).

Various tests exist for the following: clerical aptitude, vision, interest and intellectual ability. If you do not have the necessary expertise yourself, you can try approaching **recruitment agencies** and **consultants**. Rather spend a bit of money at this point than experience great frustration (and losses) later with the wrong staff. Ensure, however, that the consultant or agent has access to and uses the necessary evaluation methods and that the results are explained to you clearly.

CHAPTER 6
The Human Resource Function

Check the applicant's references
Any relevant information that is not yet known can be obtained from previous employers or referees. (A referee is a person whose name the applicant provides and from whom you can obtain more information on the applicant.) Such information can be obtained by telephone, personal letter or personal visit. This step is essential to determine the credibility of the applicant, and should therefore not be neglected. You can learn much from previous employers. Remember, however, to 'read between the lines' in your conversation with referees. They may often gloss over important defects in an applicant's character.

Conduct the employment interview
Plan and arrange for the interview and tell the applicant where and when it will be held. Make sure that you are familiar with all the necessary facts. Prepare the questions that you want to ask. Try to determine whether the person will be **suitable** and will **get on** with the other employees and with you. This is particularly important if you will work closely together. Look at the whole person and remember that no-one is perfect. Look for **good and bad points** and ask yourself whether you could find a more suitable person. **Past performance** is usually a good indication of what to expect in the future.

Examples of questions that you could ask:
- Why are you applying for the post?
- How do you view your role in the business?
- How can you see yourself contributing towards making the business more productive?

Have the applicant undergo a medical examination
The candidate must be physically suitable for the job to be done. If there is any problem, it should preferably be identified in good time. High medical claims and absentee figures will thereby be avoided.

Make the final employment decision about whom to employ
Decide who you will appoint in the job. Be objective and remember that you are looking at the work to be done, and not at the person. Write a letter and make an offer to the candidate chosen, giving a starting date, the salary and other benefits attached to the post.

THE ENTREPRENEURSHIP SERIES
Management for Entrepreneurs

DO: Write down the questions you would ask during an employment interview for the post 'senior administrative officer'. The person will have three subordinates.

....
....
....
....
....

The applicant must now decide within a given time whether to accept the offer or not. The offer can also be negotiated. Negotiability will depend on you. Conclude a **contract** with the employee. The contract usually contains the basic policy and conditions of service of the business. Working hours, leave, overtime and so on are usually specified in this document.

If the offer is not accepted, the next most suitable candidate is considered. Once the chosen candidate has accepted the offer and informed you of the decision, you can embark upon the induction process and start to motivate the person.

5.3 Employment

The employee presents himself or herself at the business on the agreed date and administrative matters are finalised. The necessary forms, such as unemployment insurance, tax and medical aid forms, are completed. (See 'remuneration' below for further information.) Open a **personal file** for the new employee. This is simply a file in which you keep all the person's documentation, personal information and correspondence. You may need such documentation later for matters such as promotion, dismissal, transfer and merit assessments.

5.4 Induction

Induction is the process in which employees are introduced to:
- the business, procedures, environment and working situation;
- their co-workers and boss.

CHAPTER 6
The Human Resource Function

This is an opportunity that you should use to motivate new employees and put them at ease. There are many benefits for the business in the long term if new employees understand well from the start how the business works and can communicate effectively with other people in the business.

To make a new employee productive and happy as fast as possible, draw up a list of what you should do:

- **before** the employee arrives at the business;
- on the **first day**;
- during the **first two weeks**;
- during the **first six months**.

The following are a few recommendations. You will probably be able to add others to this list.

Before a new employee arrives at the business

Congratulate the person. Send the successful applicant a formal **letter of welcome** and an **information brochure** on the business. Information such as the following is usually appreciated: working hours, dress code, schools and estate agents in the area, and general policy of the business.

Ensure that the person's **office or work space** is in order and that the necessary furniture, equipment and stationery are in place before he or she arrives. Inform **other employees** about newcomers and what work they will be doing.

On the first day

Make sure that you are available to **meet** newcomers and to introduce them to the other employees. Chat a little with new employees to put them at ease. Show every employee to the office or work space where he or she will work. Finalise **administrative matters** such as the completion of the necessary forms. Get each newcomer **working** as soon as possible. Appoint someone to orient the newcomer or do it yourself. Check whether the person has **transport** to work and **accommodation**.

During the first two weeks

The newcomer is now systematically introduced to the following:

- The activities of the department and how it supports the business as a whole;

- ❏ The employee's **duties** and **responsibilities** (refer to job description);
- ❏ How, where and when employees are **paid**;
- ❏ **Working hours, leave, meal** and **tea-times**;
- ❏ The use of the **telephone**;
- ❏ **Dress code**;
- ❏ **Recreation facilities**.

During the first six months

To ensure that the potential of the newcomer is used to the optimum, induction does not end after a week or two. You should ensure that the employee **develops**. **Identify** his or her **training needs** and see that the **training** takes place.

> Draw up an **induction programme** for newcomers to your business. Divide it into four parts as explained above. Be specific so that you can use it as a working document.
>
> BEFORE THE EMPLOYEE ARRIVES
> ....
> ....
>
> ON THE FIRST DAY
> ....
> ....
>
> DURING THE FIRST TWO WEEKS
> ....
> ....
>
> DURING THE FIRST SIX MONTHS
> ....
> ....

CHAPTER 6

The Human Resource Function

6 MOTIVATION

An induction programme is a good start to ensure that your employees are motivated. The idea of motivation is to get your employees to **want to deliver their best** in the work situation.

Many people say that they are motivated by money. This may partly be true, but it does not tell the whole story. Think, for instance, of what you would do to teach your dog to perform the command 'sit'. The only way to achieve this is to give the dog a biscuit or other form of reward. But there must be more than simply the reward: what about the sitting action? In each case **you** are the one who is motivated to make the dog sit. And when you come to the end of your biscuits, you have nothing more to motivate the dog. If you use only money to motivate your employees and your motivational fund runs low, you will easily lose them.

> **There are two types of factors you must look at, namely:**
>
> ❑ Factors outside the work;
> ❑ Factors concerned with the work itself.

The **factors outside the work** are, for instance:

❑ Salary;
❑ Job security;
❑ Working conditions;
❑ Organisation policy and procedures;
❑ Quality of supervision;
❑ Interpersonal relationships at work.

You should ensure that these factors are fairly acceptable in your business. Only when this is the case can you pay attention to the following set of factors.

The factors that deal with **the work itself** are:

❑ Performance;
❑ Recognition;
❑ Responsibility;
❑ Promotion;
❑ Opportunities for growth in the work.

THE ENTREPRENEURSHIP SERIES

Management for Entrepreneurs

You must create an environment in which employees can grow and function to their full potential. This means, for instance, giving them recognition for good work, more responsibility and creating opportunities from which they can grow, progress and use their full potential.

You should therefore ensure that you know your employees. Each has different needs and views on the work. The same factors do not apply to everyone, and not everyone has the same personal objectives. Your relationship must therefore be such that you know what motivates each one and is important in each case. For instance, there are employees who would rather grow in the work itself than be managers. Promotion will therefore not necessarily motivate such employees.

DO

What factors motivate employees? Make a summary of the section you have just worked through by writing down keywords below.

FACTORS APART FROM THE WORK	FACTORS CONCERNED WITH THE WORK ITSELF
....	....
....	....
....	....
....	....
....	....
....	....
....	....

7 TRAINING AND DEVELOPMENT OF STAFF

When you appoint new staff, remember that as new employees they will not necessarily be well prepared to do the work, although they may have attended a college or technikon or have worked before. Each business differs and it will be necessary to train the newcomer in the policy, procedures and practices of your business. The training process begins as soon as you start your induction programme.

You may wonder, perhaps, what the difference is between training and development.

CHAPTER 6
The Human Resource Function

Training is a systematic, planned process to change employees' behaviour, attitude, working habits and possibly levels of job performance with the purpose of making them more effective in their current posts.

Development is a process aimed at the systematic preparation of employees with potential for certain management posts. It is a process in which managers and potential managers acquire the necessary skills and attitudes to function successfully as managers.

In a small business you will not have to do much development but, if necessary, you can enrol those with management potential on management courses. Such people will then be used as supervisors and possibly later as managers of various departments. Within the business you can start giving such people more responsibilities and delegate more management functions to them. Keep an eye on them, give them advice and help them to prepare themselves for possible promotion. It is naturally in your own interests and those of your business to have good supervisors and managers. Remember, however, that you yourself must also keep developing to be successful.

Training must always provide for a specific need and must not be done simply for its own sake.

When you wish to **draw up a training programme**, you can use the following steps:

❑ **Determine training needs.** Establish whether your employees need training, and exactly what form of training they need.
❑ **Establish objectives for the training programme.** Write down what you wish to achieve with the training. Be specific and use standards.
❑ **Determine the type of training programme.** Do the employees need basic training (such as training in the use of the telephone), or more specific training (such as training in a new computer program)?

- **Determine suitable training methods.** Will you use lectures, in-service training, videos, case studies or other methods? Here you will also have to decide whether you will do the training yourself. If not, will you get someone to do it internally, or will you send employees to an outside training centre? Remember, you may know the business, but you will not always have the necessary skills to be able to give your staff the best training. In such a case you can therefore work together with external people. They will also not know the business, and you will therefore have to give them the necessary background.
- **Present the training or send employees for the training.**
- **Evaluate the training.** Determine whether the set objectives have been achieved. If not, you will have to reassess the trainer, method, objectives and standards.

You have decided that the book-keeping system in your business should be computerised and that all transactions must take place directly on computer. The accountant in your business, David, is not familiar with the relevant program and will have to be trained. How would you set about training him?

....
....
....
....
....

REMUNERATION

Money is probably the factor that motivates most employees to apply to work in a specific business.

Your **remuneration policy** should be in line with the remuneration for similar work in other businesses. You will periodically have to adjust salaries or wages to keep up with the rising cost of living and inflation. This should also enable employees to maintain a realistic standard of living and to make sufficient provision for the future.

CHAPTER 6
The Human Resource Function

To draw a distinction between the productive employee and one who does as little as possible, employees may be paid per job or by the quantity of work. This is known as the **piece-wage system**. An amount is therefore paid once the specific job or piece of work is finished. A worker may, for instance, be paid R20 for every zip replaced in a pair of trousers, irrespective of how long the job takes.

Indirect remuneration or **fringe benefits** vary from business to business. These are types of remuneration that employees receive in addition to their salaries. You may, for instance, pay a portion of employees' total pension for them, or give them housing subsidies. These benefits are not necessarily given to all employees. Certain fringe benefits are given only to workers above a certain level in the hierarchy.

Another example of a fringe benefit is when you deduct employees' medical aid contributions from their salaries **before** you pay them. The payment to the medical aid is then not indicated on the salary slip. The benefit is that the payment to the fund is done before taxation of the employees' salaries, and because their tax deduction is calculated on a slightly smaller amount, they pay less tax.

Another example is profit sharing. If profit is higher than a certain amount, you may, for instance, pay out 2% of the profit once a year to employees. This makes employees feel that they have a personal interest in the business, which has a motivating effect.

The question now arises of **how much** to pay a specific employee.

When deciding on a salary, you can use the **following guidelines**:

- It is good first to look at the salary of **similar posts** in other businesses.
- Compare the value of the posts in other businesses with the value of the post in your business. This is known as **job appraisal**.
- Place the posts in **sequence** from the employee on the lowest level to the employee on the highest level.
- Finally, draw up a **remuneration policy** and attach a salary scale to every level in the business.

Look at the following example of a salary scale:

SALARY SCALE FOR 'OWN SHOP CC'

POST LEVEL 1:	CLEANER/MESSENGER	R12 000 – R24 000
POST LEVEL 2:	SALESPERSON PACKER CLERK/SECRETARY	R15 000 – R50 000
POST LEVEL 3:	SENIOR CLERK	R24 000 – R98 000
POST LEVEL 4:	SUPERVISOR	R60 000 – R120 000
POST LEVEL 5:	CO-DIRECTOR	R100 000 – R200 000

Other factors that will determine how much you pay your employees are:

- supply and demand of labour;
- your ability to pay;
- the prevailing minimum wage.

It is good to draw up a remuneration policy. You may decide to use consultants to help you with this. **Employees must be informed about the policy** and they must know why they are placed on a certain level.

When you pay your employees, there are also other aspects you should look at. Your business should be registered with the **Receiver of Revenue**. It is your responsibility to deduct tax from the salaries of your employees and to pay this monthly to the Receiver. (This must take place according to tables obtainable from the Receiver.) At the end of the tax year (28 February) you must give each employee an IRP5 form. (This is a summary of the employee's income during the past year and the deductions from her/his salary.) All employees must be registered with the Receiver of Revenue and must have a tax number.

You must also register your business with the **Unemployment Insurance Fund**. This you can do at the nearest Department of Labour office. In 1995 the deduction for this fund was 1% of an employee's salary. The same amount must then also be paid into the fund by your business. This deduction applies to all employees who earn less than a certain salary (the amount in 1995 was just under R70 000 a year).

Remuneration can be paid monthly as a **salary** or weekly or daily as a **wage**. A salary is usually paid to permanent employees, or to temporary

CHAPTER 6
The Human Resource Function

employees appointed for a certain period. A wage is usually paid to employees who are not appointed permanently.

If you are not sure what to do, consult the Receiver or the Department of Labour. It is better to ask in time than to realise later that you were wrong.

Deduct all the **calculated deductions and fringe benefits** from the employee's salary and pay them to the relevant institutions. Examples are tax, pension payments, medical aid contributions, subsidies and allowances. You should also arrange for the **physical payment** of wages and salaries in the form of cash, cheques or direct payment into a bank account. All employees must also receive salary slips. If you wish to pay your employees physically in cash, remember that it can be a problem transporting large quantities of cash, and that robberies are a risk of this form of payment. For control purposes and the purposes of evidence, an extra person should always be present to witness a cash payment.

> Draw up a **remuneration policy** for your business. Ensure that all the points mentioned above appear in the policy.
>
> ....
> ....
> ....
> ....
> ....

Instead of making use of employees, you can also use **contractors** to get the job done, and pay them in a similar manner as for the piece-wage system.

Let us assume you have a job to be done and you want to make use of contractors. This job could be a one-off, such as getting someone to paint your shop, or it could be on a continuous basis, as when you get someone to manufacture shoes for you in the long term.

The first thing you have to do is come to an agreement with the contractor about the job to be done and the amount payable for the job. Then you must draw up a contract, both parties must accept the contract and sign it together with two witnesses. The contract must state the following:

- ❑ **Details of service or the product to be provided.** This is the job or task that is expected from the contractor. Sometimes it is necessary

to include a lot of detail, so that both parties understand exactly what the contract entails. The type of job can also be a service.
- **Machines, materials, stock and maintenance.** Here it must be stated who will provide what and the standards involved.
- **Fee structure.** The amount you will pay for the completed work, for each completed section of the work or for specific services rendered.
- **Dates** of commencement and completion of the job.
- **Breakdown or any other hold-up.** Discuss the consequences and actions.
- **Indemnity, guarantees, liability and insurance, any legalities, and safety and security rules and regulations.**

As mentioned, the contractor is not an employee and does not have the same rights and advantages as an employee. For example, the contractor cannot have paid leave, must pay her/his own medical aid fees and must cater for her/his own pension and insurance. The contractor is in fact working independently for herself/himself and is in no way part of the enterprise for which the work is being done.

9 LABOUR RELATIONS

Labour relations are concerned, among other things, with the drawing-up, maintenance, change and administration of rules, control processes, ideologies, interaction and relations in the workplace.

The labour relations system is a threefold relation between labour, management and the government.

Figure 6.3

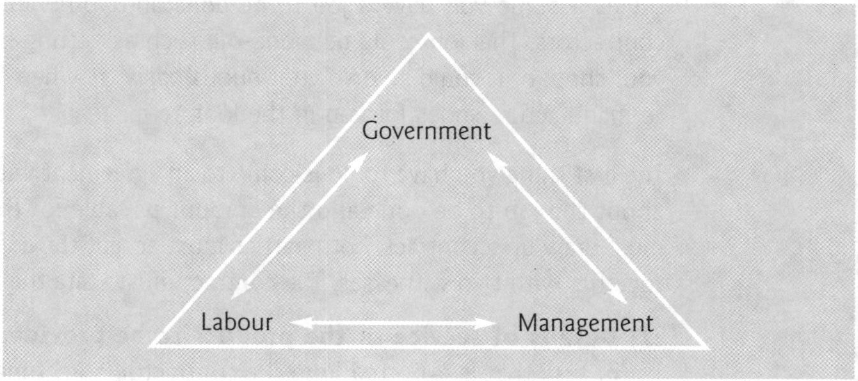

CHAPTER 6

The Human Resource Function

Each of these three groups has its own interests and needs, and it is inevitable that conflict will sometimes occur. An example of conflicting interests is the wage question. Workers would naturally like to ensure that their wages are as high as possible, while management, on the other hand, would like to make as much profit as possible and therefore does not want to pay excessively high wages.

It is in your own interests, and also in the interests of employees, to try to achieve a conflict-free climate. Any conflict that may occur must then be settled in the prescribed way.

When you deal with **trade unions** you should always be familiar with the various Acts that regulate labour relations. The Department of Labour is responsible, among other things, for administering the following Acts:

- The Labour Relations Act 66 of 1995;
- Basic Conditions of Employment Act 75 of 1997;
- Occupational Health and Safety Act 85 of 1993;
- Compensation for Occupational Injuries and Diseases Act 130 of 1993;
- Public Holidays Act 36 of 1994;
- Employment Equity Act 60 of 1998;

Contact one of their offices if you wish to know more about any of these.

When employees have a problem or a grievance, there must be channels by which they can bring this to the manager's attention. A **grievance procedure** is therefore drawn up to be followed in such a case. This sets out in clear steps who should be addressed about the problem and what employees should do if the problem cannot be solved.

The same type of procedure is set out for cases of disciplinary action against an employee. **Disciplinary procedure** may take one of the following forms, in order of seriousness:

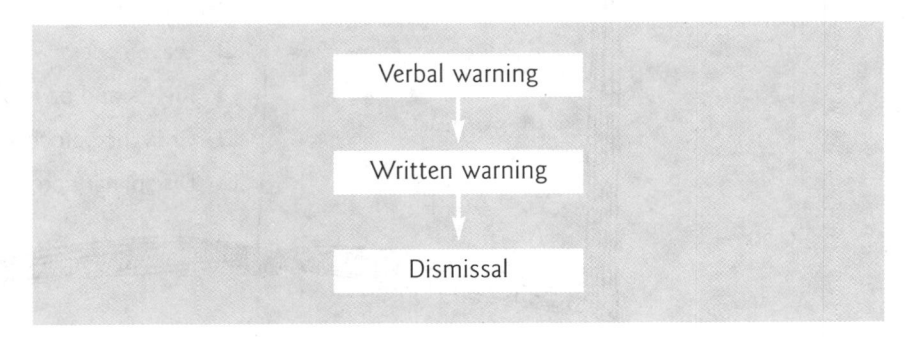

Verbal warning
↓
Written warning
↓
Dismissal

THE ENTREPRENEURSHIP SERIES

Management for Entrepreneurs

Disciplinary steps are taken when an employee breaks certain set rules of conduct.

However, labour relations is a very comprehensive subject and, as you may study it as an additional option, we will not deal with it in any more detail here.

> How would you discipline an employee who is often absent and who causes the work to run late?
> ....
> ....
> ....
> ....

10 OTHER FACTORS

Finally, we will look at a few other factors that you can keep in mind with regard to human resource management. It is a good idea to draw up a **policy document** setting out the following: conditions of service, leave codes, rights and privileges of employees, and grievance and disciplinary procedures. This document must be available for all employees. If you have just one or two employees, you may be able to manage without it, but it will come in handy when your staff increases. It offers you a guideline for dealing with certain conduct, ensures that your conduct is consistent and guarantees that everyone is familiar with procedure.

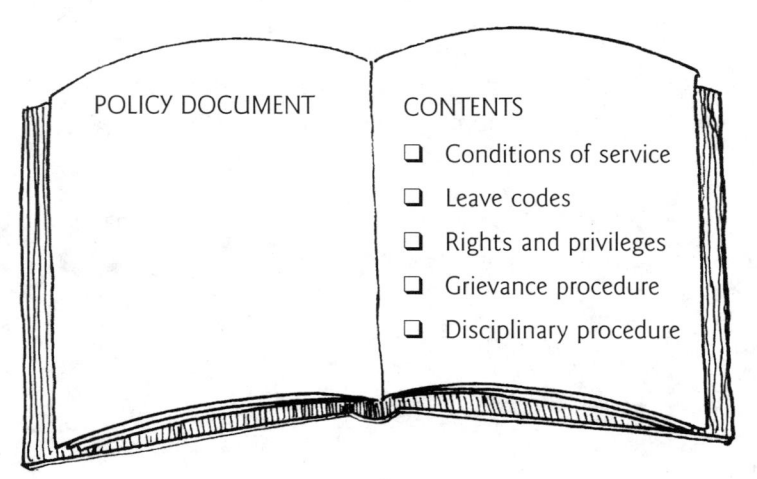

POLICY DOCUMENT

CONTENTS
- ❑ Conditions of service
- ❑ Leave codes
- ❑ Rights and privileges
- ❑ Grievance procedure
- ❑ Disciplinary procedure

CHAPTER 6
The Human Resource Function

Unsafe, unhygienic and unpleasant working conditions may cause employees to be injured or get ill. This will result in them being off work more and in lowered productivity and reduced profit. Employees may also lay a charge against you if they are injured on duty. Ensure, therefore, that conditions are safe and that employees observe the rules of safety. If your business is such that a lot of dangerous work is involved, contact the National Occupational Safety Association (NOSA) for advice.

> Write down topics that you think should be addressed in your enterprise's business policy.
> ....
> ....
> ....

11 SUMMARY

Many staff matters will require your attention. The fewer employees you have, the easier it should be, but if you expand and your staff increases, you will have to look at possibly appointing someone to deal with all these matters. Remember, you can also appoint someone temporarily or on a half-day basis. You need to ensure that these administrative duties do not take up too much of your time, since this could have a detrimental effect on your business.

12 SELF-EVALUATION

Read the case study below and answer the questions that follow.

> A few years ago you started a sole proprietorship. Initially you had a seamstress make denims for you and you sold these over weekends at flea markets. This went so well that you decided to open a shop. The seamstress cannot handle the demand and you need to employ two others. You also need an accounting officer to help you with the financial side of the business.

1. Draw up a job description for the accounting officer.

   ....
   ....
   ....

2. Draw up an advertisement for the post of the two seamstresses you require. The advertisement will appear in the local press.

   ....
   ....
   ....
   ....

3. Draw up a remuneration policy for your business.

   ....
   ....
   ....

4. Your sister's friend does not have a job. She would like to help you make clothes, but does not know much about needlework.

   (a) You decide to employ her. How would her induction programme differ from that of a person who can sew?

   ....
   ....
   ....

   (b) You realise that you cannot use her. How would you handle the matter?

   ....
   ....
   ....

5. You decide to expand and also to sell shoes. Explain the implications of this for your human resource planning.

   ....
   ....
   ....

REFERENCES

Beach, D.S. 1985. *The Management of People at Work.* 5th edition. New York: Macmillan.

Bekker, F. & Staude, G. 1988. *Starting and Managing a Small Business.* Cape Town: Juta.

Le Roux, E.E. et al. 1999. *Business Management: A Practical and Interactive Approach.* 2nd edition. Johannesburg: Heinemann.

Quible, Z.K. 2000. *Administrative Office Management – An Introduction.* 7th edition. Englewood Cliffs, New Jersey: Prentice Hall.

Scarborough, N.M. & Zimmerer, T.W. 2000. *Effective Small Business Management: An Entrepreneurial Approach.* 6th edition. New York: Macmillan.

7 THE ADMINISTRATIVE FUNCTION

1 LEARNING OBJECTIVES (OUTCOMES)

After you have studied this chapter, you should be able to:

- Explain what the administrative function entails;
- Explain the difference between data and information;
- Identify and describe the steps of information management;
- Determine the information needs of a small business;
- Identify and briefly explain the administrative sub-systems in a small business;
- Develop internal and external mail procedures in a small business;
- Develop a filing system for a small business;
- Describe financial record-keeping in a small business;
- Explain how the computer can be useful in a small business.

2 INTRODUCTION

The owner or manager of a small business must have usable information to make good decisions. The administrative function plays an important role in this regard, since it is concerned mainly with the **provision of usable information**.

The administrative function renders a service to the other enterprise functions such as the human resources function, the financial function and the marketing function, by supplying information with which decisions can be made. It also entails **ordinary administrative tasks** such as:

- the handling of mail;
- filing;
- telecommunication services;
- printing and copying;

CHAPTER 7
The Administrative Function

- certain aspects of book-keeping;
- costing;
- managing budget systems;
- keeping business statistics.

Administrative tasks differ from one business to another and are influenced mainly by the **size and type of business**. A person selling clothing at a flea market, for example, will not have as extensive a filing system as someone selling flower seeds to all nurseries in the Gauteng region.

In larger businesses, a **central administrative department** usually handles the administrative tasks. You can also use such a department when you expand your business. In smaller businesses, however, **single individuals** handle most of the administrative tasks.

> Write down for yourself any administrative tasks that may be involved in running a business.
> ....
> ....
> ....
> ....

INFORMATION MANAGEMENT AS A COMPONENT OF THE ADMINISTRATIVE FUNCTION

Information is the heart of decision-making in any enterprise. Incomplete or insufficient information is often the cause of wrong decisions and can lead to loss of money, time and labour and even the failure of your enterprise. The provision of the **right information** at the **right time** and in the **right form** is essential for the survival and success of your enterprise. Before we can have usable information, we have to process the available data. You have probably wondered whether there is a **difference between data and information**.

> **Data are facts in an unprocessed form** which cannot be used in the decision-making process in that form; for example, a pile of invoices of all sales for the year.

177

THE ENTREPRENEURSHIP SERIES
Management for Entrepreneurs

> **Information refers to the data that have been processed** so as to be usable in a specific situation; for example, the invoices arranged in chronological order, or a comparison of the number of products sold last month with the figures for the same month the previous year.

Take a look at the example below illustrating data and information.

Assume the owner of a home industry wants to determine whether it is worth opening on Sunday mornings. To make a profit she will have to sell baked products worth at least R1 000.

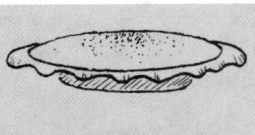

The following were sold one Sunday morning:

$$\left.\begin{array}{lll}\text{25 chocolate cakes} & @ & \text{R12,50} \\ \text{10 milk tarts} & @ & \text{R8,50} \\ \text{12 chicken pies} & @ & \text{R6,30} \\ \text{13 carrot cakes} & @ & \text{R15,00} \\ \text{10 dozen sausage rolls} & @ & \text{R7,00}\end{array}\right\} = \text{DATA}$$

If the owner of the home industry wants to determine total sales for the day, she has to process the above data.

$$\left.\begin{array}{llllll}\text{25 chocolate cakes} & @ & \text{R12,50} & = & \text{R312,50} \\ \text{10 milk tarts} & @ & \text{R8,50} & = & \text{R85,00} \\ \text{12 chicken pies} & @ & \text{R6,30} & = & \text{R75,60} \\ \text{13 carrot cakes} & @ & \text{R15,00} & = & \text{R195,00} \\ \text{10 dozen sausage rolls} & @ & \text{R7,00} & = & \underline{\text{R70,00}} \\ & & & & \text{R737,50}\end{array}\right\} = \text{PROCESSING}$$

$$\left.\begin{array}{l}\text{Sales of R737,50 were made on the Sunday} \\ \text{morning. If average sales on Sunday mornings} \\ \text{remain R700,00, it will not pay the owner} \\ \text{to open on Sundays.}\end{array}\right\} = \text{INFORMATION}$$

If the owner wants to determine at a certain stage how many items of specific baked products are sold, she will have to develop a simple system for herself. For example, she can attach a code to each item and type it into the cash register before entering the price.

CHAPTER 7
The Administrative Function

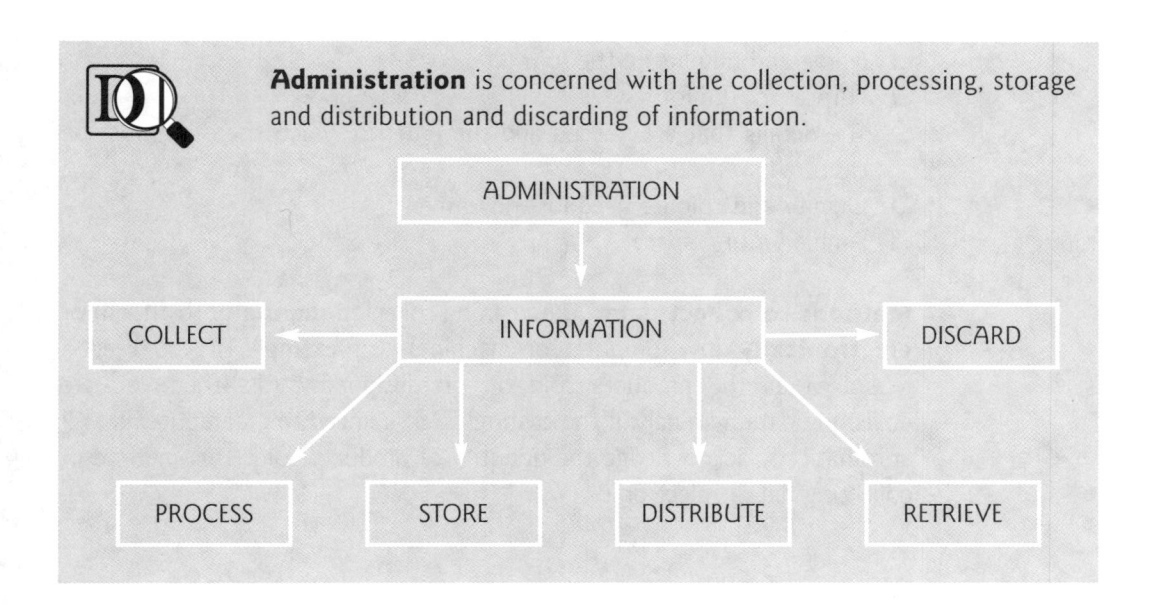

Administration is concerned with the collection, processing, storage and distribution and discarding of information.

```
                    ADMINISTRATION
                          |
                          v
  COLLECT  <----     INFORMATION     ---->  DISCARD
                   /    |      \
                  v     v       v      v
              PROCESS  STORE  DISTRIBUTE  RETRIEVE
```

3.1 Collection of data

A business can collect data from inside (**internal**) or outside (**external**) the business. The business has no control over the format and type of data available from outside the business. Data from inside the business can be collected in specific forms, because you have more control of the processes inside the business. A business would like to receive information on all aspects that effect its work. Therefore a decision must be taken on what types of information need to be received.

When collecting data, there are three aspects to consider: the specific activities of the business, the format of the data and the methods used to collect it.

Activities on which data must be collected: The owner/manager of the business must decide for which activities it is necessary to collect data: for example, the recording of sales transactions, payments made and products produced.

The format in which to collect data: Data can be recorded in a systematic way on pre-designed forms. Normally, a pre-designed form would include the following:

❏ Name and number of the form;
❏ Purpose of the form;
❏ The details that are needed and the order in which the data must be captured;
❏ Quality and colours used for the form;
❏ Ample writing space.

Methods to collect data: Data can be collected **manually** (by hand) or **electronically** (by computer or machine). For example, if you keep a record of all the products sold on pre-designed cards, then you are collecting data manually. If the cash register is linked to a computer, it will automatically acknowledge the quantity of products sold. This method of collecting data is electronic.

3.2 Processing of data

Before the data can be processed, it must **first be made usable**. It is therefore necessary to classify, group and sort the data.

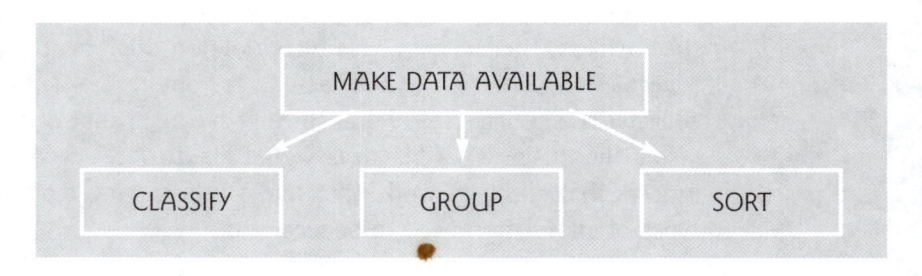

```
                    MAKE DATA AVAILABLE
                   ↙          ↓          ↘
            CLASSIFY       GROUP         SORT
```

Classification consists of arranging the data according to a specified characteristic in order to place it in meaningful **groups**. For example, you can collect the purchasing invoices and then classify sales according to region or salesperson. **Sorting** refers to arranging the data in some way, such as placing invoices in sequence by date or number.

Data can be processed **mechanically**, for example by a computer, or **by hand**. Examine Figure 7.1, which represents a computer-based data processing system, and Figure 7.2, which represents a hand-based system.

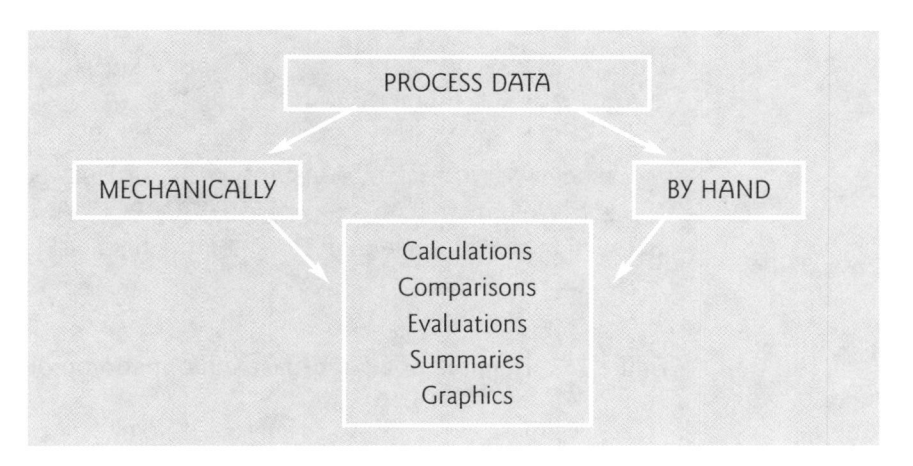

CHAPTER 7
The Administrative Function

```
                    PROCESS DATA
                   /            \
        MECHANICALLY              BY HAND
                   \            /
                    Calculations
                    Comparisons
                    Evaluations
                    Summaries
                    Graphics
```

Data can be processed by making calculations, drawing comparisons, doing evaluations, making summaries and creating graphics. **Calculations** are done using mathematical principles. To give an employee a monthly pay slip, for example, an owner must multiply the employee's wage rate by the number of days worked, minus tax and other deductions. **Comparisons** are done, for example, by comparing the stock levels and order quantity of a certain item with each other.

Figure 7.1 Example of a computer-based information processing system

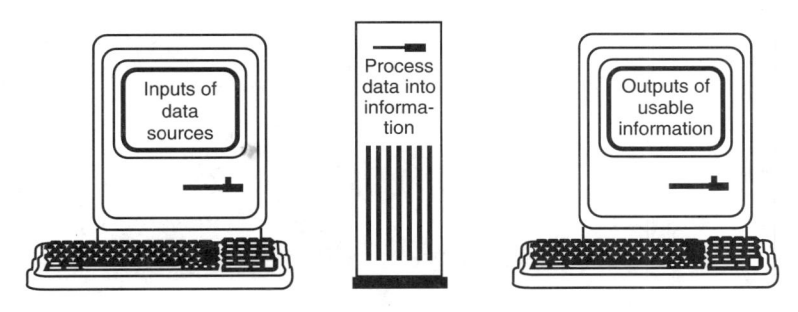

[Inputs of data sources] → [Process data into information] → [Outputs of usable information]

Assume the owner of a liquor store wants to know how much stock he has of a specific drink. For this he will use the computer. The stock quantities of all the drinks are available on the computer, because the liquor store owner enters this information on the computer each month (it is the INPUT).

He selects the specific drink, and the computer searches for the information in its memory (PROCESSING).

THE ENTREPRENEURSHIP SERIES
Management for Entrepreneurs

> After a few seconds the available stock requested by the owner appears on the computer screen (OUTPUT).
>
> After the owner has seen the quantity of available stock, the computer stores the information on its hard disk (STORAGE). At the end of each transaction the information is stored on the hard disk.

Figure 7.2 Example of a hand-based information processing system

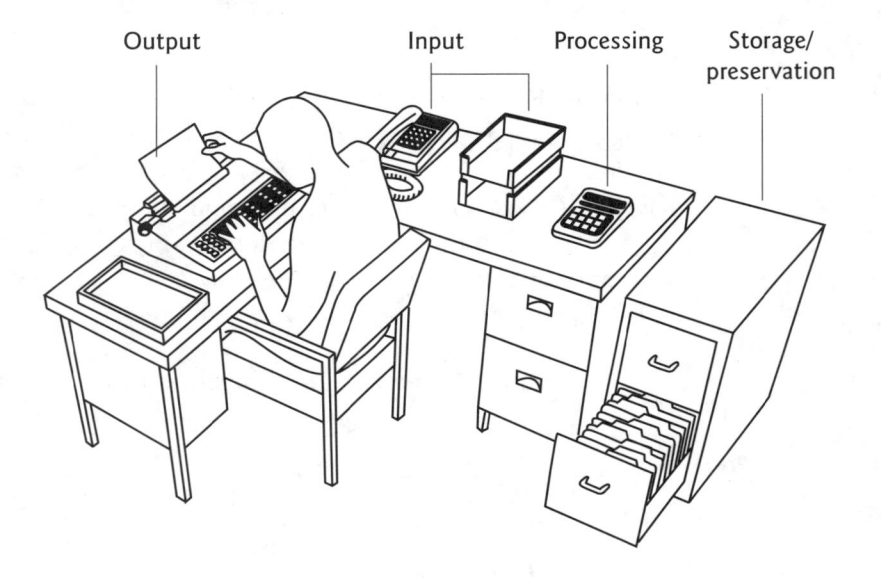

Output   Input   Processing   Storage/preservation

> A secretary has obtained quotations for photocopiers because the business wishes to purchase one. She now collects all the documents, notes and information she has received by telephone (INPUT).
>
> She sums up the data and works out the costs against the amount budgeted for purchase of a photocopier (PROCESSING).
>
> The secretary gives this report to the owner (OUTPUT).
>
> After the owner has read the report, he files it for later reference or use (STORAGE).

CHAPTER 7
The Administrative Function

3.3 Storing and retrieving

Information can be stored for short or long periods, manually or electronically. Information that is stored manually is usually placed in cabinets, shelves or file holders specially designed to store paper documents. Information stored electronically is usually put on a computer system. In all instances, a **filing system** is necessary to be able to **recall** (retrieve or get) the information. Fixed rules should be developed to guide the filing of documents; without rules, it becomes very difficult to retrieve documents when you want them. (We will discuss filing in section 5.5.)

Information that has been efficiently created and stored is of little value unless it can be retrieved when needed. **Retrieving information** is the process of locating the stored information. In a manual system, you will get the information from the shelf, cabinet or file where you have stored it. In an electronic system, you will retrieve the information from the computer where you have stored it.

❑ Write down what storing and retrieving method you are currently using in your business.

....
....

❑ Do you think this method is successful? Give a reason for your answer.

....
....

3.4 Distribution of information

The data that have been processed into information must now be made available to the people who will use it. Information can be **distributed** in many ways: for example, conversation, telephone, letters, reports and electronically by means of computers or fax machines.

Examples of information products are the budget, financial statements and computer printouts.

THE ENTREPRENEURSHIP SERIES
Management for Entrepreneurs

3.5 Discarding of information

Discarding (throwing away) information means the deliberate physical destruction of documents or files that no longer have any value to the users. Documents can be destroyed manually by throwing them in a waste bin, by means of a paper shredding machine or by burning. In an electronic system, information can be discarded at a touch of a button on the computer keyboard.

Before you destroy any information, you must determine what the retention requirements are. For example, you may think that you do not need your financial statements any more, but the law determines that you must keep your financial records for a certain period of time.

> **DO:** Find out what the retention time is for all legal documents in South Africa. If you are aware of this information it could be of great assistance when you want to determine what information must be destroyed.

Look at the following example that illustrates the five steps of information management in a business.

> **eg:** Busy Bee Store collects the following sales data available for the first six months of 1999, 2000 and 2001.
>
> | MONTH | 1999 | 2000 | 2001 |
> |---|---|---|---|
> | January | R20 000 | R30 000 | R26 000 |
> | February | R18 000 | R26 000 | R25 000 |
> | March | R19 000 | R28 000 | R20 000 |
> | April | R19 000 | R25 000 | R21 000 |
> | May | R20 000 | R22 000 | R23 000 |
> | June | R19 000 | R21 000 | R20 000 |
>
> The above data must be processed to be useful. We can do this by calculating the average sales for the first six months of each year.

CHAPTER 7

The Administrative Function

MONTH	1999	2000	2001
January	R20 000	R30 000	R26 000
February	R18 000	R26 000	R25 000
March	R19 000	R28 000	R20 000
April	R19 000	R25 000	R21 000
May	R20 000	R22 000	R23 000
June	R19 000	R21 000	R20 000
TOTAL	R115 000	R152 000	R135 000

A comparison can be made from this information. We can see that 2000 was the most successful year in terms of sales because more products were sold.

Busy Bee Store can store this information electronically (e.g. by means of a computer) or manually in a filing cabinet. Because this information is properly stored it would easily be retrieved.

Information must be made available to the people who will use it. In this case it will be the sales manager. The sales information can be presented (distributed) to the sales manager in a table form or as a graphic in a report.

Sales for 1999	Sales for 2000	Sales for 2001
R115 000	R152 000	R135 000

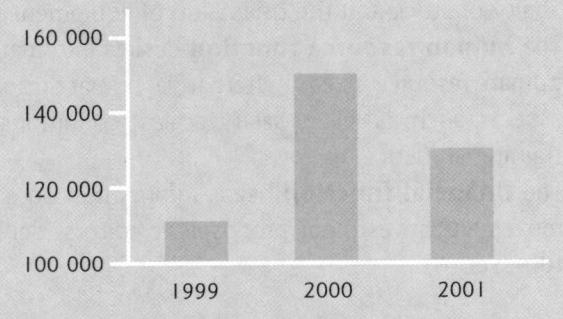

If Busy Bee Store does not need this information after several years, it can be discarded manually or electronically.

We will now consider the different information needs that can arise in a small business.

4 THE INFORMATION NEEDS OF A BUSINESS

In small businesses where the owners are also managers, they are constantly aware of what happens in the work situation. If the business sells products, for example, and resistance to the product occurs, the owner-manager can make efforts based on personal experience to adapt the relevant product to the new demands.

As we said in the introduction, the administrative function renders a service to the other enterprise functions. These functions all need their own type of information. We will mention several examples of each.

- The **owner/manager** needs information on the general financial position and profitability of the business, and on the technological developments and performance of other functional areas.
- The **marketing function** would like information on clients and potential clients, their spending capacity, geographic location, markets, market segments and needs. Information is also needed on competition, prices, alternative forms of marketing communication, sales volumes, sales values and marketing costs.
- The **purchasing function** would like information on existing and potential suppliers, quality and prices of raw materials and equipment, acquisition costs, stock levels and consumption rates.
- The **production function** is interested in information on the budgeted and actual production volumes, production costs, the availability of stock and the utilisation of equipment and staff.
- The **human resource function** desires information on the business's human resource needs, alternative human resources, and personnel aspects such as leave, salary scales, conditions of employment and training statistics.
- The **financial function** needs information on capital sources, capital movement, investment proposals, creditors, debtors, stock levels and turnover.

Apart from the legal obligations to publicise certain information, you will have to provide particular information to certain parties in their dealings with your business.

CHAPTER 7
The Administrative Function

Such interest groups include the following:

- **Capital providers** such as banks are interested in information on your enterprise's solvency and liquidity. Solvency is the business's capacity to pay its debts at any time – its total assets must cover the total liabilities of the enterprise. Liquidity is the business's capacity continuously to make all payments regularly and on time.
- **Suppliers** are interested in the creditworthiness of your enterprise to determine whether you can pay them.
- If you have **employees**, they will want information on their conditions of service.
- **Consumers or clients** are interested in all information on the business's products.
- A great range of information is required by the **government**. Information must be given mainly to the following bodies: the Receiver of Revenue, the Compensation Commissioner, the Unemployment Insurance Fund and the Registrar of Companies.

As you can see, therefore, there are many kinds of information that your business will either have to supply, or will have to obtain at some time, for you to make meaningful decisions.

Write down the information needs of your business. This will prepare you to establish systems and procedures to satisfy these needs.

....
....
....
....
....

ADMINISTRATIVE SYSTEMS

A system can be described as a number of mutually dependent sub-systems, parts or procedures that work together towards a common goal or function.

If we make this description applicable to the administrative function in a business we can illustrate it as follows:

THE ENTREPRENEURSHIP SERIES
Management for Entrepreneurs

```
                    Administrative system
                            |
         Sub-systems of the administrative system
                            |
    ┌───────────┬───────────┬───────────┬───────────┐
 Telephone    Mailing   Reprographic  Records    Financial
  system     system      system      management  record-keeping
                                     system      system
    └───────────┴───────────┴───────────┴───────────┘
                            |
    Each of these sub-systems has its own procedures and methods
```

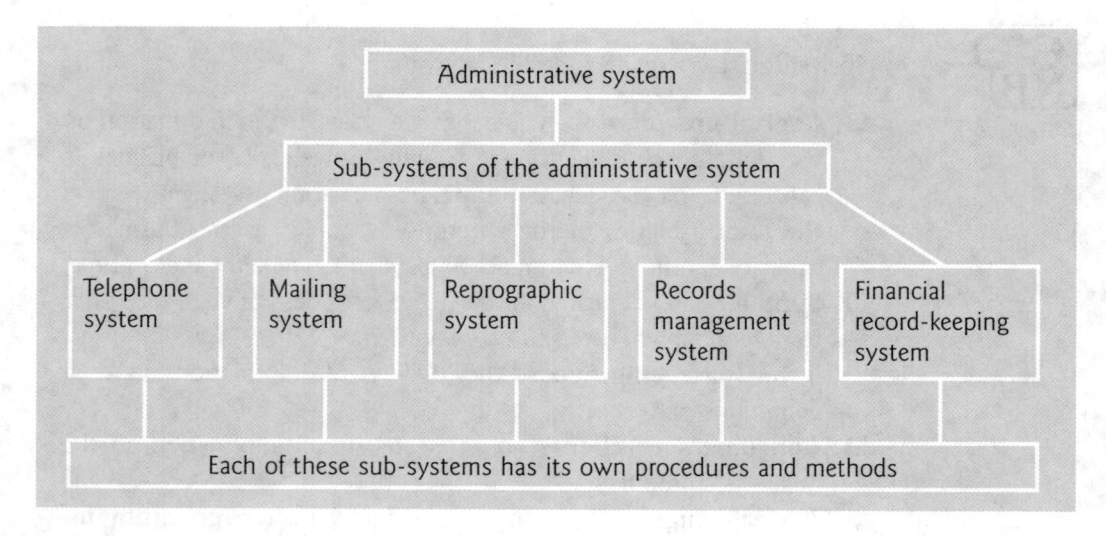

As a small business owner/manager, you will have to set up each of these systems to ensure the smooth running of your business. In this section we will briefly cover the most important things to consider when setting up these sub-systems.

5.1 Telephone system

The telephone is perhaps the most important piece of business equipment. Businesses use telephones to make first impressions, sell products, provide customer service and negotiate contracts.

The volume of telephone calls will determine the kind and size of system that you need. A small business may have only one telephone with one local line. As the business expands, however, it will need more telephones and a greater number of lines, which will require the use of a larger system.

Depending on your needs, a wide range of services and features can be added and adapted to a business telephone system. These services and features can be categorised as basic, advanced and customised.

Basic features
These include the following services: automatic callback, call forwarding, call waiting, speed calling and intercom.

CHAPTER 7
The Administrative Function

Advanced features
- Visual displays built into phones make them easier to use because the instructions for use are given by means of a pre-set menu.
- Electronic directories store many numbers and names in the memory of your telephone for easier dialling.
- Call logging stores incoming call information and provides a complete record of calls for quick return calls.
- Fax switch recognises an incoming fax call and automatically directs it to your fax or modem.
- Call waiting display allows you to see who is calling even while you are on the phone by displaying the caller's number and/or name after you hear the signal tone.
- Deluxe call waiting allows you to select one of the five options for a call waiting, voice mail, send a wait message, send a busy message, conference or drop.

Customised features
Particular telephone problems can be solved by customising some of these special features: for example, forwarding calls when you are elsewhere and fax, modem, business and personal calls on one line. You sometimes need more than one phone line and often more than one phone for each line or you need a separate line for fax/modem transmissions.

5.2 Postal mailing system

Most businesses rely heavily on communication with their customers and clients. Efficient mail systems must be designed and set up to ensure cost-effectiveness and efficiency, thereby delivering better service to customers. If your business deals promptly with correspondence, this will contribute to the punctual execution of orders, safe handling of money and negotiable documents, immediate attention to complaints and thorough control over all staff activities.

Incoming mail
The size and nature of your business will determine how the incoming mail must be handled.

A possible procedure for handling incoming mail is the following:

a) Receive the mail and open all envelopes with a paperknife.

b) Stamp all letters and commercial papers with a **date and number stamp**, because the date of receipt is very important in the event of a dispute or delay.
c) All money, cheques, postal orders and bills are recorded in a special book, namely the **remittance register**.

Figure 7.3 Example of a remittance register

Date of receipt of money	Person from whom money is received	Nature of remittance	Amount	Signature of mail clerk	Number of receipt issued	Signature of cashier
Oct 11	Ms A du Rand PO Box 123 Alberton	Cheque	R250,00	R Lubbe	K1689	L Reddy
Oct 12	Mr G Brits	Postal order	R100,00	R Lubbe	K1690	L Reddy

d) All the mail items must then be **sorted** into different baskets. In a small business there are five main baskets:

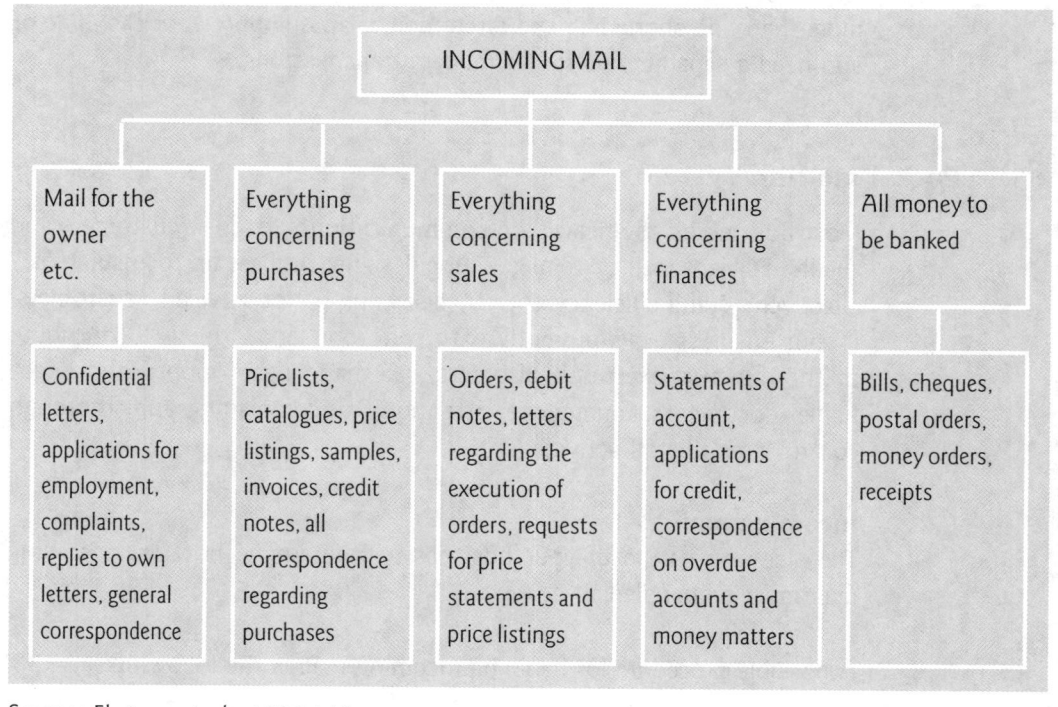

INCOMING MAIL

Mail for the owner etc.	Everything concerning purchases	Everything concerning sales	Everything concerning finances	All money to be banked
Confidential letters, applications for employment, complaints, replies to own letters, general correspondence	Price lists, catalogues, price listings, samples, invoices, credit notes, all correspondence regarding purchases	Orders, debit notes, letters regarding the execution of orders, requests for price statements and price listings	Statements of account, applications for credit, correspondence on overdue accounts and money matters	Bills, cheques, postal orders, money orders, receipts

Source: Eksteen *et al.*, 1986:147.

CHAPTER 7
The Administrative Function

Perhaps you do not need all the above-mentioned baskets in your business, but they give a good indication of how to sort mail logically. This may be useful when you expand your business.

e) Record all items of mail you receive, for example in a **letters register**. In this way you will exercise good control over incoming mail and ensure that all matters receive attention and are finalised.

Figure 7.4 Example of a letters register

Date from	No. Received	Contents	Given to	Replied	Sent
Sept 1	1 Krynauw and De Beer	Enquiry re prices of materials	Dealt with personally	2/9	3/9
Sept 3	2 NPK Dealers	Enquiry re balance balance	Secretary	4/9	6/9

Outgoing mail

The outgoing mail in most businesses consists of letters, orders, invoices, debit notes, credit notes, accounts, cheques, bills, receipts, price lists, catalogues and parcels.

How will you set about handling your outgoing mail? Here is a possible procedure:

a) Reply to all letters received as soon as possible (remember always to indicate reference numbers).
b) Indicate in the **mail register** that the correspondence has been dealt with and the date this was done.

Figure 7.5 Example of a mail register

Amount received	Date mailed	Name	Address	Description	Time	By whom	Stamps
R10,00	Aug 10	K Smit	De Aar	Letter	10:00	P.S.	R0,60
	Aug 10	R Roos	Molteno	Letter	12:00	P.S.	R0,60
	Aug 11	E Nagel	Bethal	Letter Balance	16:00	P.S.	R0,60 R8,20
R10,00							R10,00
R8,20	Aug 30	Balance					

THE ENTREPRENEURSHIP SERIES
Management for Entrepreneurs

c) When your business is such that you must send out accounts, you must do it consistently each month at the same time – or develop a policy for yourself on this and inform your clients about it.

d) Large numbers of account statements or receipts are posted mainly in window envelopes to which stamps or imprints are applied by a franking machine.

e) All the letters and their replies must now be filed in their folders in chronological order.

DO

1. Why is it beneficial to put a date and number stamp on all incoming mail?
   ....
   ....

2. For what do we use the following?

    (a) Remittance register ....
    ....

    (b) Mail register ....
    ....

3. How would your business benefit from using e-mail?
   ....
   ....

E-mail

Electronic mail (e-mail) is one of the most wonderful ways of communicating quickly with other people in a business or, for that matter, anywhere in the world. In simple terms, electronic mail is like a giant digital post office that conveys written messages anywhere in the world in a fraction of time. Users send messages via their computer screens to which a receiver can react immediately.

Some of the advantages of using e-mail are that you can:

❑ be more efficient;
❑ communicate more effectively;

CHAPTER 7
The Administrative Function

- reduce your costs dramatically (especially paper costs);
- improve your customer service;
- improve turn-around times with both clients and fellow workers.

The **Internet** connects millions of people in all parts of the world via electronic mail. To reach them, you obviously need to have an Internet connection.

Much the same etiquette that applies to writing letters today applies to electronic mail. Generally you need to be polite, considerate and precise when sending e-mail messages.

E-mail etiquette
- Check for e-mail messages every day. Senders expect immediate replies or may think that the message has not been received and send another one.
- For security reasons, do not send any messages by e-mail that you do not want anybody else to read.
- E-mail letters are just the same as letters sent through the postal system, and should be checked for typing, spelling and grammatical errors and corrected.
- Always check that your e-mail is correctly addressed.
- Keep quotes as brief as possible, but long enough to make your point.

5.3 Reprographic system (photocopying)

Photocopiers have become a necessity for most businesses, and these machines are widely used to make copies of documents and to circulate correspondence to others.

Photocopiers are available in an enormous range of configurations, from complex, high-volume printing machines to small desktop units suitable for making a few copies of documents every day. Improvements in technology have meant that other services, such as facsimile and high-quality printing, can be added to the traditional photocopying machine.

The basic operating procedures vary from one model to the next, and it is a good idea to familiarise yourself with the features offered by the particular model you use.

Purchase or hire

Because technology improves and changes so fast it is probably no longer worth purchasing a photocopying machine. When you purchase, you limit yourself, and in time you will sit with an old product that no longer satisfies your needs and that nobody will want buy off you.

The other choice is to lease. A supplier leases you the machine you require, and in exchange you pay a certain amount every month. The machine remains the property of the supplier or lessor.

Equipment is usually leased for a specific period. The period is determined by the speed of technological change. After the lease period expires, you can follow one of the following options:

- Leasing for a further period;
- Upgrading of the machine and an extension of the lease;
- Leasing a new machine in place of the old one;
- Cancellation of the lease agreement.

The lease agreement also has tax benefits. The amount is currently tax-deductible.

If you decide to purchase a photocopy machine, it is a good idea to use the machine first for a trial period before purchasing it to determine whether it is the one you want.

Photocopy machine control

When using a photocopier, it is necessary to exercise strict cost control. Here are a few suggestions in this regard:

- Make only as many copies as are necessary or were requested.
- Set the equipment so that the minimum of pages will be damaged.
- Print on both sides of the paper where possible.
- Use external printing companies if they can offer cheaper reprography.
- Buy paper in bulk if it is cheaper.
- Always check that there is sufficient paper and toner of the correct size and colour in stock for the work that must be done.
- Be aware that certain documents may not be copied: for instance, paper money, copyrighted works, immigration documents, share certificates, traveller's cheques, postal/revenue stamps and vehicle licenses.

CHAPTER 7

The Administrative Function

> Do you think it is necessary to obtain a photocopying machine for your business? Why?
>
> ....
>
> ....
>
> Make a list of uses for a photocopying machine in your business.
>
> ....
>
> ....

5.4 Records management system

Records management refers to the administrative sub-system in any business that is responsible for creating and maintaining systematic procedures and control of all the records in the business. For the purpose of this chapter we will focus on the storing (filing) of records in a business. A record refers to the written or spoken proof of information gathered and kept for use in making decisions.

5.5 Filing

> **Filing** is the way in which all documents and files are systematically stored so as to facilitate their further use for internal reference and inquiries.

Every business, whatever its size, must keep a record of its correspondence and documents. Even individuals keep a record of their personal documents in some fashion; for example, you put all your bank transactions or all your policies in one file. The most important documents we store are surely those concerned with the Receiver of Revenue. We do this so that at the end of the tax year we do not have difficulty gathering the necessary information.

Similarly, you must have some form of filing system in your business for decision-making, reference or inquiries.

There are **various methods of filing**. We will refer briefly to all these methods. It does not matter which method you choose, as long as it works for you and meets your needs.

> Before you look at the methods of filing, however, you must keep in mind the following aspects of the filing system you choose:
>
> ❑ **The needs of your business:** All businesses handle a large number of documents daily, and it is therefore important that you use a filing system that will meet the needs of your business. For example, if you have a hair salon, you can use a card system on which you write the name and contact telephone number of each client, together with the details and date of whatever treatments they receive.
> ❑ The filing system must be one that **can grow and expand with the business**. It must be possible to enlarge it without costing the business much extra.
> ❑ The filing system must **work in a simple way** so that the user can gain easy access to it in tracing and storing any files and documents (except confidential documents).
> ❑ The **place and equipment in which documents are stored** must be durable and fire-resistant so that the documents and files are well preserved for a long time. It must be possible to store the documents safely without the danger of their being damaged, stolen or destroyed by fire.
> ❑ A filing system **must not occupy much space**. The less space it occupies, the more money you save, because every square metre you use costs money.

Now let us consider the methods of filing.

CHAPTER 7

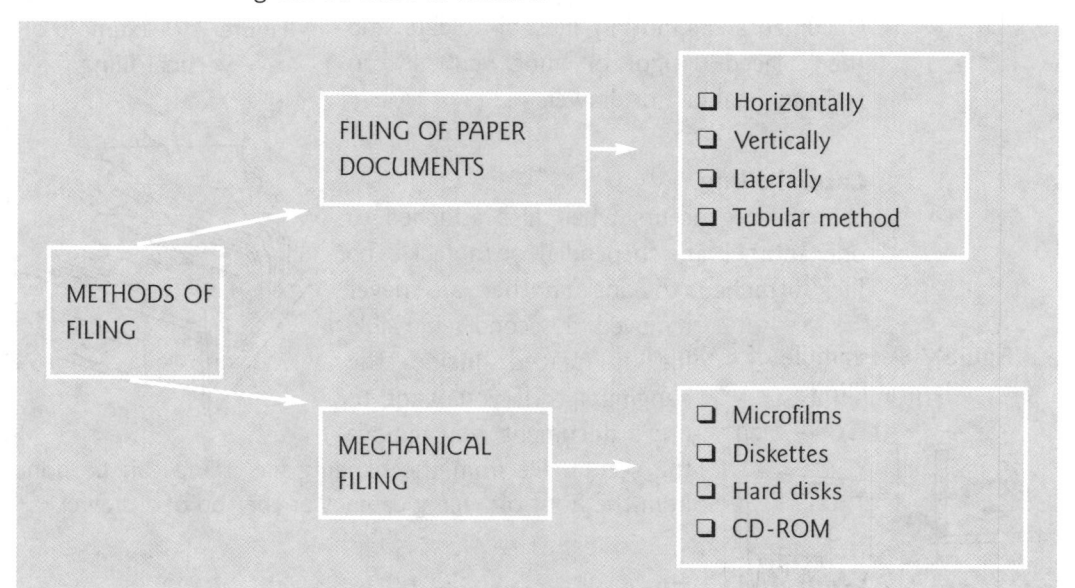

The Administrative Function

Filing can be done as follows:

METHODS OF FILING
- FILING OF PAPER DOCUMENTS
  - ❑ Horizontally
  - ❑ Vertically
  - ❑ Laterally
  - ❑ Tubular method
- MECHANICAL FILING
  - ❑ Microfilms
  - ❑ Diskettes
  - ❑ Hard disks
  - ❑ CD-ROM

5.6 Filing of paper documents

Horizontal filing

This is the most basic way of storing documents and files. The files or documents are simply **stacked flat on top of one another** in a pigeon-hole or on a spike. At predetermined times they are collected, sorted, classified and grouped. The documents are then done up in bundles, with the description of the contents on each, and stored in cupboards. The pigeon-hole is particularly useful in the filing of forms such as cash slips, invoices, debit notes, credit notes, bank deposit slips and so forth.

Figure 7.6 Pigeon-hole

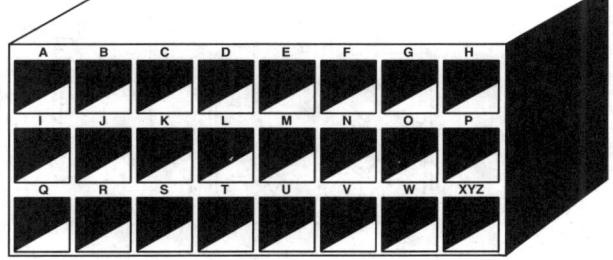

Vertical filing
Documents are put in files or folders and then placed upright or hung vertically on racks in a cabinet or drawer.

Lateral filing
Lateral filing occurs when files attached to one another are suspended on a rack. The files attached to one another are never removed; a second removable file is placed inside the hanging file. If you want to use a document, you remove the second file from the hanging file. Filing can be done from the front of a filing cabinet or the top of a drawer.

Figure 7.7 Example of vertical filing

Figure 7.8 Example of lateral filing

Filing using the tubular method
Documents that are too large to fit into files are rolled up and stored in tubes. These tubes are usually made of hard cardboard, metal or plastic. The name of the document is written on the lid of the tube. Documents normally stored using the tubular method are house plans, engineering drawings, sketches and so on.

Most documents are printed on paper and can therefore be stored using one of the above methods. **However, there are also mechanical means of storing information.**

Figure 7.9 Example of filing using the tubular method

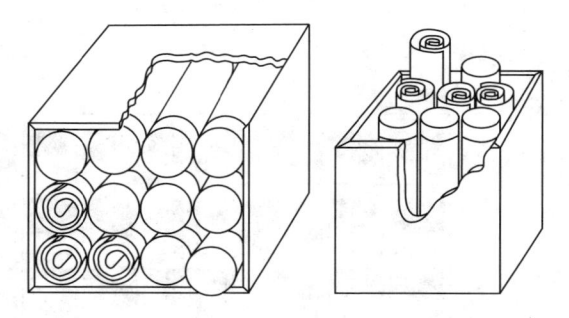

CHAPTER 7
The Administrative Function

5.7 Mechanical filing

Microfilm

A microfilm looks like the negative of a photograph but is slightly larger. Hundreds of pages of information can be put on one microfilm. The information is photographed by a special camera, and the images are reduced and put on a microfilm. A **microfilm reader**, which looks very like a television screen, is used to enlarge the microfilm and to display documents on a screen. This method of filing saves a great deal of space.

Each microfilm is clearly marked. Documents on microfilm cannot be rearranged. Microfilm is numbered chronologically and filed. Banks and shops use microfilm mainly to refer to the balances on clients' accounts.

It is very unlikely that a young small business would use this method of filing. However, we have mentioned this method because it is certainly an option that can be considered when you expand your business or if your business is concerned with reference works, the supply of information to other businesses, and so forth.

Figure 7.10 Example of a microfilm slide and microfilm reader

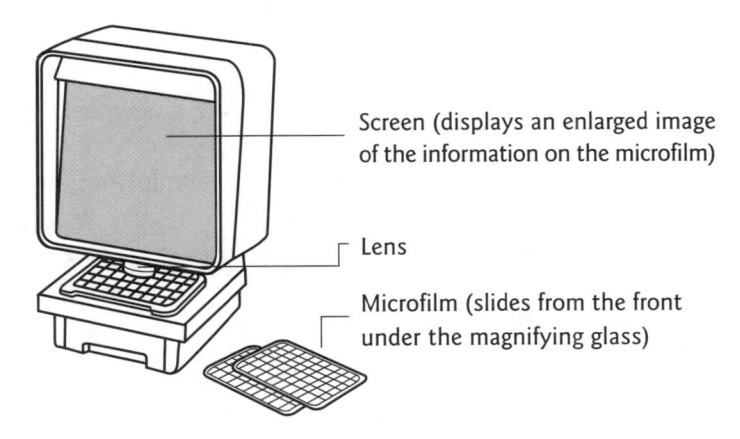

Screen (displays an enlarged image of the information on the microfilm)

Lens

Microfilm (slides from the front under the magnifying glass)

Diskettes and hard disks

Information is stored by a word processor on a magnetic disk or on the hard disk of a computer or word processor. The information can then be called up or changed later.

Figure 7.11 Filing of information on diskette

THE ENTREPRENEURSHIP SERIES
Management for Entrepreneurs

DO

1. List the methods that can be used to file paper documents.
   ....
   ....
   ....

2. Which filing method would you use in your business? Why?
   ....
   ....
   ....

5.8 Filing equipment

The technology in this regard changes and evolves constantly, and consequently new filing equipment appears on the market virtually every day. When you have decided on the method you will use for filing, it would be wise to inquire from the suppliers of office equipment concerning available filing equipment. You can even look in second-hand shops for this equipment. Sometimes you find such equipment in good condition at half the price of the new item.

Examples of filing equipment are shown below.

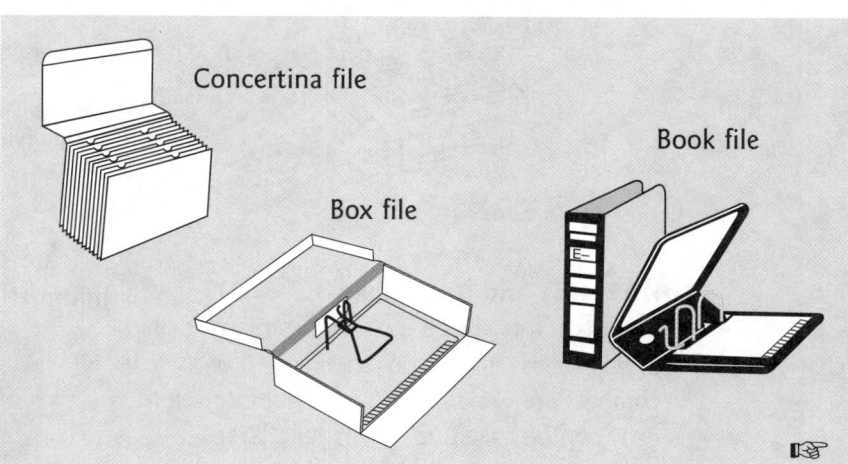

Figure 7.12 Examples of filing equipment

CHAPTER 7

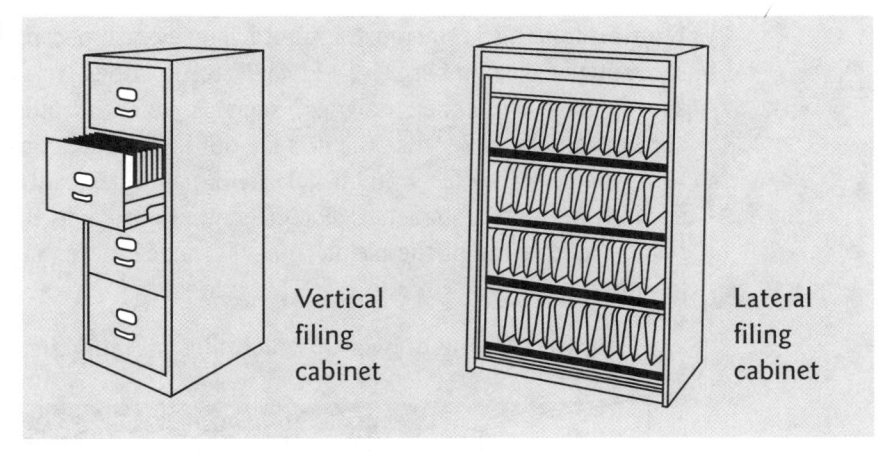

The Administrative Function

Vertical filing cabinet

Lateral filing cabinet

5.9 Classifying and arranging of files

When you choose a filing system, you must decide how the files are going to be classified and arranged. There are various methods of doing this:

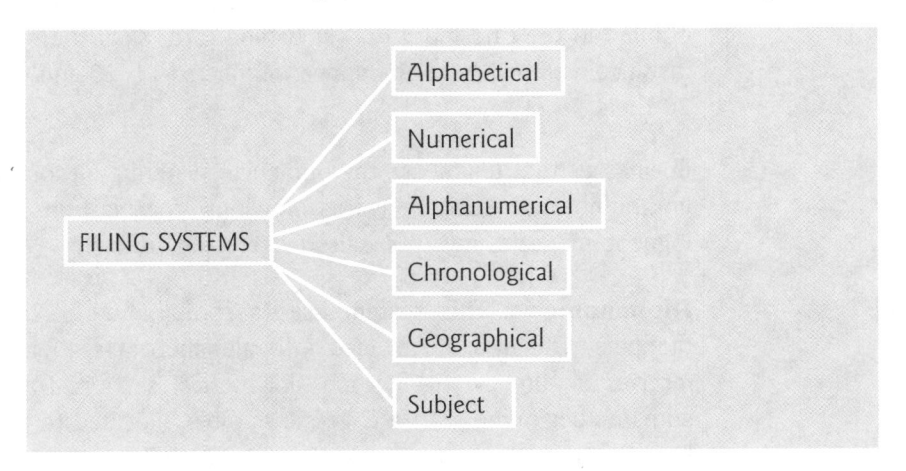

FILING SYSTEMS:
- Alphabetical
- Numerical
- Alphanumerical
- Chronological
- Geographical
- Subject

Alphabetical: Files are kept under the names of individuals, businesses or government organisations and filed by the sequence of letters in the alphabet. This system is most commonly used in businesses. When you use an alphabetical filling system it is helpful to get to know the rules of alphabetical filing.

Figure 7.13 Alphabetical filing

201

Numerical: This is the most accurate filing system because items are filed sequentially by number: 1, 2, 3, 4, 5 etc. It is best used for items that already have a number assigned, such as purchase orders or customer account numbers. Because the files are not filed alphabetically, it is difficult to remember every file's number. Therefore an index card system must be used. This is an alphabetical list of content on cards that contains the number and name of the client. This card index makes it easier to search for a particular file.

Figure 7.14 File drawer in which files are numerically arranged

For example, if you want to remove D. Khumalo's file, you look up the number in the card index drawer behind card 'K'. If the number is 20, for instance, you will go to the drawer numbered 11–20 and trace file number 20 there.

Businesses that might use the numerical system are those which need to link numbers to such things as drawings, specifications, factories, catalogue items, sales invoices, sales ledgers and so forth.

Alphanumeric: This system uses a combination of both letters and numbers. The files are divided into alphabetical sections and each file receives a number within each alphabetical section. For example, each surname beginning with a G gets a number allocated to it. This normally happens in doctor's rooms. All the people whose surnames begin with G

Figure 7.15 Alphanumeric filing

are filed in one cabinet, but all the Gs cannot be filed alphabetically because new patients arrive daily or weekly. Therefore they get the next number allocated to them: G1, G2, G3 etc.

Business that will use this system are, for example, builders or consultants that continually get new clients. The client's files are then not arranged strictly according to surnames.

Chronological: Records are sorted in date order, usually year, month or day. This system is used specially for temporary filing and tickler or reminder files. Records that need attention in the future – a day, a week, a month or even a year ahead – are filed by the relevant date and retrieved on that date. This system is useful for scheduling daily, monthly and yearly activities and can be used by any business.

A **tickler file** works as follows: it has a series of 12 guides with the names of the months printed on tabs, and 31 guides with the numbers 1 to 31 printed on the tabs. A tickler file is generally kept on your desk. When something must be taken care of on a certain date, a card is prepared with the necessary information and placed behind the appropriate month and date. The tickler file is checked every morning to see what must be done that day.

Geographical: With this system, information is filed according to geographic location. Records are indexed using the names of cities, towns and suburbs. For example, a stationery wholesaler that operates nationally in South Africa would first do its filing by province, and then alphabetically.

Subject: Records are filed alphabetically by topic or category rather than by individual or business name. Major filing categories are: accounting, advertising, budget, credit department, inventory, personnel etc.

THE ENTREPRENEURSHIP SERIES
Management for Entrepreneurs

What filing system would be most appropriate to use in the following instances? Give reasons for your answer.

	FILING SYSTEM	REASON
A business's invoices		
Correspondence files		
A small enterprise where category headings are well known by everybody who is using the system		
A travel agent		
A list of suppliers		
A dentist		

Before filing records, they must be prepared by inspecting, indexing, coding, cross-referencing and sorting. This will ensure that the filing is done accurately and successfully.

Inspecting records
- Remove all staples and paper clips.
- Repair any damaged sheets.
- Place records together that relate to one file.

Indexing records
Indexing is the process of deciding where a record needs to be filed. In alphabetical filing, indexing means determining the name that is to be used, for example: A.J.M. De Wet and Associates (De Wet is the keyword). In subject filing, indexing means determining the most important subject discussed in the record.

Coding records
Coding is the marking of the record by the name, subject, location or number that was determined in the process of indexing. The record may be marked by underlining, circling or checking. Coding is important because it saves time in the refiling process.

One of the most helpful aids in a filing system is the colour-coding of records. The purpose of colour-coding is to answer questions about the location, content or purpose of an item without having to actually read or open it. For example, if you use the alphabetical filing system you can use a different colour for each letter of the alphabet; As in blue, Bs in red, Cs in yellow etc.

Cross-reference: Sometimes a record may need to be stored in more than one place, and this could cause problems when trying to retrieve the information. For example, say you work in the human resources department of an organisation. A memorandum has been circulated regarding changes in benefit policies: retirement, sick leave and vacation pay. You already have separate folders for each of these topics. You could make a copy for each of these files or file it in one folder – say, vacation pay – and place a cross-reference sheet in the other two folders (sick leave and retirement).

Sorting: Sorting is the arrangement of records in the order in which they are to be filed. The records should first be sorted into a few groups, then into the final arrangement. For example, in an alphabetical system all the records with the same letter are grouped together and then arranged in the exact alphabetical order. A sorter can be used to do the sorting. The guides on each flap of the sorter carry an alphabetical designation. If records are not filed immediately, it is helpful to have the material in a sorter at your desk so that they may be located quickly without having to shuffle through a pile of papers.

5.10 Tips for effective filing

- Do the filing daily; do not let it pile up.
- Work systematically when you file.
- Staple together all the documents that belong together.
- Sort the documents before filing them to speed up the work.
- Do not let the files become too full. Replace them and put old documents in the archive regularly.
- Irregular correspondence must be filed in the right place so that it can be found easily later.
- Completed files must be filed immediately to prevent misunderstandings.

THE ENTREPRENEURSHIP SERIES
Management for Entrepreneurs

- ❏ Make sure that the correct documents are in the correct files.
- ❏ Always do your filing in a consistent fashion.
- ❏ Put an 'out' card or an 'out' file in the place of a file that has been removed so that you can keep a record of who has taken the file.
- ❏ Make sure that confidential letters and documents are kept safe.

Can you think of further tips for filing? Write them down because you will definitely find them useful one day.

....
....
....
....
....

FINANCIAL RECORD-KEEPING

Financial record-keeping, together with filing, is one of the most important components of your business. Just as you have to keep a record of documents, so you must keep a record of all your financial transactions. Financial record-keeping can be regarded as **the heart of the business**. If you do not know what is happening with regard to your finances, you may as well close your business.

Financial record-keeping **gives you the necessary information to help you manage the finances of your business** and to make important decisions about its future. The information you keep acts as a permanent record of completed transactions and is evidence for the auditors that the accounting entries are correct. In addition, the law obliges you to keep some kind of record of all financial transactions.

As we mentioned earlier, you can also use a **computer** to keep a record of all your financial transactions.

Sometimes it is also more cost-effective to use a **part-time book-keeper** to deal with this side of your business. You might not be very knowledgeable about accounting and could have many other things on your mind.

CHAPTER 7
The Administrative Function

Money moves in and out of the enterprise continuously. If you do not exercise strict control over this, it will be difficult to establish whether you are making a profit or loss. What makes record-keeping so important is that no-one can remember what transactions were made on particular days, not to mention months and years. For this reason, a small business must **use at least the following financial registers to record its financial transactions**:

NB

All businesses must start with a **cash book, petty cash book** and **general ledger**.

	WHAT IS IT USED FOR?	WHEN ARE THE ENTRIES DONE?	HOW OFTEN IS IT BALANCED?
CASH BOOK	– Keeps a record of all receipts and cheque payments – Easy reference for monitoring the bank balance and cash flow – To reconcile with the bank statement of the previous month	Each day	Each month
PETTY CASH	– Keeps a record of all cash payments – To compare the cash in hand with the balance in the cash book of the previous week	Each day	Each week
GENERAL LEDGER	– Contains a record of all transactions that are divided into different ledger accounts of the business – Entries from other accounting books are transferred here	Each month	Each month

THE ENTREPRENEURSHIP SERIES
Management for Entrepreneurs

When your business expands, you can also use the following **additional accounting books**:

	WHAT IS IT USED FOR?	WHEN ARE THE ENTRIES DONE?	HOW OFTEN IS IT BALANCED?
SALES JOURNAL	– Keeps a record of all invoices issued by the business for the provision of goods and services	Each day	Each month
DEBTORS LEDGER	– Keeps a record of all clients who owe the business money, with the amount and period the money has been owed	Each month	Each month
WAGES AND SALARIES JOURNAL	– Keeps a record of all the wages and salaries paid, to whom, and the deductions made, for example income tax, unemployment insurance, pension fund and medical fund	Wages = weekly Salaries = monthly	Wages = weekly Salaries = monthly
STOCK REGISTER	– Keeps a record of the movement of stock in the business – Reconciles it with total stock in the general ledger	Each day	Each month
PURCHASES JOURNAL	– Keeps a record of all credit purchases you have made	Each month	Each month

CHAPTER 7

The Administrative Function

CREDITORS LEDGER	– Keeps a record of all suppliers to whom you owe money	Each month	Each month
GENERAL JOURNAL	– Is not often used, but provides for the alteration of entries and for entries not usually made in the other journals	Each month	Each month
ASSETS REGISTER	– Keeps a record of all fixed assets in the business, together with the depreciation and the profit and loss	Each month	Each month

Why is it necessary to have a system for financial record-keeping?

....

....

....

7 USE OF THE COMPUTER IN A SMALL BUSINESS

Computers have come to play a vital role in handling information, for the following reasons:

❏ Computers are so much **cheaper** for storing and distributing information compared to the old paper systems with their enormous postal and filing components.
❏ They have the ability to **speed up commercial transactions**, which causes assets to be used more productively and clients to react more swiftly.

209

THE ENTREPRENEURSHIP SERIES

Management for Entrepreneurs

> ❏ They **make information that has already been gathered easily available** for a secondary use. For example, if your inventory system is computerised you can establish at any time how much of any product is available and when to order new products.

Examples of where the computer can help you in your business are the following:

- ❏ Book-keeping;
- ❏ Salaries and wages;
- ❏ Word processing;
- ❏ Storage of documents;
- ❏ Lists of all your clients to whom accounts and information must be mailed;
- ❏ Price lists;
- ❏ Catalogues;
- ❏ Quotations;
- ❏ Filing;
- ❏ Lists of suppliers with all their details;
- ❏ Pre-formatted forms such as invoices, memorandums, debit notes and credit notes;
- ❏ Standard letters;
- ❏ Stationery such as letterheads;
- ❏ Design of handbills;
- ❏ Reports;
- ❏ Graphic designs and much else, depending on your specific need.

When you use a computer, you do not have to know about the mechanical composition and operation of the computer. The software programs you will use can teach you, or you can appoint someone in your business to do the computer work for you.

These days there are also many consultants who can advise you on what computer and software to acquire for your specific needs.

CHAPTER 7
The Administrative Function

The advantages of the computer in a small business environment are the following:

- More and better information is obtained for making decisions.
- More timely information is available.
- Information is more accurate.
- It reduces boring, routine work such as book-keeping.
- It improves client service.
- It improves internal control.
- It increases the productivity of employees.
- It can improve the production processes.

Unfortunately, computers also have certain disadvantages, such as the following:

- A computer is very expensive to acquire.
- A computer bought today could be obsolete tomorrow.
- The variety of software available on the market makes it difficult to decide on a specific package
- Costly mistakes can be made when using the computer by entering incorrect data and information into it. The results (output) will then also be incorrect.
- Managers can rely too much on a computer and later expect it to make decisions for them. Small business entrepreneurs must realise that the computer is only a resource to support them in solving problems and making decisions.

By improving the gathering of information and by creating information, computers can help to save small businesses from failure.

Can you use a computer in your business? If so, what will you use it for?

....
....
....
....

THE ENTREPRENEURSHIP SERIES

Management for Entrepreneurs

8 SUMMARY

The administrative function makes information available to the owner-manager of a small business. This information is indispensable for the management of the business. The administrative function also provides a service to all the other functions in the business as regards the supply of information, as well as general administrative tasks such as the handling of mail, filing, telecommunication services, printing and copying, aspects of book-keeping, costing, the budget system and business statistics.

The information made available must be applied usefully to assess the profitability of the business.

9 SELF-EVALUATION

The two owners of a restaurant divide their tasks as follows: one is responsible for the general management, reservations, bar and liquor purchases; the other concentrates on everything concerning the kitchen, all purchases for creating the dishes and the restaurant's book-keeping.

In the reception area the counter is always messy, with papers of all kinds lying around, such as orders, invoices, receipts and price lists.

It has already happened several times that clients have ordered a dish on the menu and that it has not been available. The clients have then had to be satisfied with their second or even third choice.

Answer the following questions:

1. What do you think is the main reason for the chaotic conditions in the restaurant?

   ....
   ....

2. How can the owners use a computer to facilitate their management task?

   ....
   ....
   ....

CHAPTER 7
The Administrative Function

3. What filing method and system would you recommend for the restaurant? Why?
   ....
   ....
   ....
   ....

4. Give the restaurant owners some guidelines on how to do better filing.
   ....
   ....
   ....
   ....

5. What financial records on the restaurant do you think they should keep?
   ....
   ....
   ....
   ....

6. Do you think keeping a mail register will help the restaurant owners in the management of their restaurant? How?
   ....
   ....
   ....

REFERENCES

Eksteen, F.R.L.N., Naudé, C.H.B., Miller, H.R. & Eksteen, F.R.L. 1986. *Business Economics for Standard 8*. Cape Town: Nasou.

Eyre, E.C. 1989. *Office Administration*. London: Macmillan.

Harrison, J. 1987. *Office Procedures*. London: Pitman.

Horsfall, M. & Cairns, S. 2000. *Office Skills, A Practical Approach*. 2nd edition. Roseville: McGraw-Hill.

Keeling, B.L. & Kallans, N.F. 1996. *Administrative Office Management*. 11th edition. Cincinnati: South-Western.

Korf, E. 1994. *Office Practice NSC*. Johannesburg: Lexicon.

Le Roux, E.E. (ed.) 1995. *Business Economics: A Practical Approach*. Johannesburg: Lexicon.

Marx, X., Van Rooyen, D.C., Bosch, J.K. & Reynders, H.J.J. (ed.) 1998. *Business Management*. 2nd edition. Pretoria: Van Schaik Publishers.

Marx, S. & Rademeyer, W.F. 1990. *Bedryfsekonomie. Volume 2*. Pretoria: Van Schaik Publishers.

Marx, F.W. & Van Aswegen, P.J. (eds) 1984. *Business Economics: A Short Survey*. Pretoria: Haum.

Odgers, P. 1997. *Administrative Office Management. Strategies for the 21st Century*. Cincinnati: South-Western.

Scarborough, N.M. & Zimmerer, T.W. 1993. *Effective Small Business Management*. 4th edition. New York: Macmillan.

Technikon SA. 1990. *Office Administration III*. Florida: Technikon SA.

Wilson, D.A. 1994. *Managing Information*. Oxford: Heinemann.

Wright, C. 1995. *Successful Small Business Management in South Africa*. 6th edition. Sandton: Struik Business Library.

8 THE PUBLIC RELATIONS FUNCTION

1 LEARNING OBJECTIVES (OUTCOMES)

After you have studied this chapter, you should be able to:

- define public relations;
- identify the objectives of public relations in the business world;
- identify the various interest groups (publics) of your business or prospective business;
- evaluate the importance of public opinion;
- explain how important public opinion is to a business;
- distinguish between the various methods of communication;
- describe what 'social responsibility' involves.

2 INTRODUCTION

As a small business entrepreneur, you have many things to consider before starting your business. For instance, before you decide on a site, purchase stock or appoint staff, you must first investigate the area and decide what the attitude of the inhabitants will be towards a business such as yours.

NB: When we talk of the area or environment and of the public or interest groups in this chapter, remember that these are groups affected directly or indirectly by the small business.

As any successful entrepreneur knows, the area or environment plays a very important role in the success and growth of a business. If feelings in the area are opposed to the establishment of a specific business, such as a pub or restaurant, the business will not be supported and is doomed to failure. The support of the public unfortunately cannot be purchased along with the rest of the stock – it must be 'earned' and maintained, and it is here that **public relations** is involved.

As you already know, various functions of the enterprise must also be considered when you set up a business. In large organisations a separate department head manages each of these functions. Public relations is one of the functions of the enterprise.

> Can you recall what the other functions of the enterprise are? Write them down below.
> 1. ....
> 2. ....
> 3. ....
> 4. ....
> 5. ....
> 6. ....
> 7. ....
> 8. Public relations..

In smaller businesses all these activities still take place, but, because the business is small, the activities are coordinated and there is not a separate department for every function. Owners or managers themselves are responsible for the smooth functioning of the business activities, and they are therefore also responsible for ensuring a good **image** for their businesses.

It is important to remember that **staff** are also responsible for protecting the good name of the business. Think of the way in which the secretary answers the telephone, or the contribution that a person working in production makes to the quality of the product or service. In other words, everyone is involved in presenting the image of the business. Remember, the employees also benefit if the business is successful.

How important is this function really?

No business, however large or small, can exist in isolation.

People, both inside and outside the business, who may be involved either directly or indirectly (see section 5), react to the 'message' or image that the business conveys.

CHAPTER 8

The Public Relations Function

Because any business is dependent on the goodwill of the public, it is important for the owner to take account of the public. The way in which a business establishes its image can be compared with a jigsaw puzzle. Every message sent out to the public is like a piece of the puzzle. To complete the puzzle, each piece must fit. If the pieces are fitted incorrectly, the picture is not clear, and the owner's expectations are then not met. Often people will later say that a business was unsuccessful because the entrepreneur's idea of the business was not viable, when in fact the owner may simply not have paid enough attention to the interest groups.

As an entrepreneur, you should pay attention to interest groups in the following ways:

- Note consumers' preferences;
- Note the new strategies of competitors;
- Care for the welfare of employees.

Because employees are one of the interest groups in a business their welfare should also be taken into account to ensure that they in turn have an interest in the welfare of the business.

If you as an entrepreneur care for the welfare of staff and treat them well and fairly, your staff will be happy. They will tell friends and family how well they are treated, and in this way your business will acquire a positive image.

Responsible entrepreneurs know that the environment plays a very important role in the success and prosperity of their businesses. For instance, if the public is opposed to some of the products sold by a dealer, such as dangerous toys or toy guns, the dealer may have to consider removing these products, or be prepared to forfeit some customer support.

As we have said, such customer support unfortunately cannot be bought with the rest of the stock, but must first be earned and then maintained.

THE ENTREPRENEURSHIP SERIES
Management for Entrepreneurs

Public relations is therefore the function that aims at creating a good image for a business among all the people or businesses that have an interest in the business.

1. Sometimes two entrepreneurs have the same type of business, but one is more successful than the other. After reading the last few pages, can you explain this?

   ....
   ....
   ....

2. Give two examples of how employees can convey a good image of the business at which they work.

   ....
   ....

DEFINITION OF THE FUNCTION

Public relations is very important in gaining public support for a small business. This leads to the following question:

WHAT does public relations involve?

In simple terms, public relations involves the relationship between the entrepreneur and those people who have an interest in his or her business.

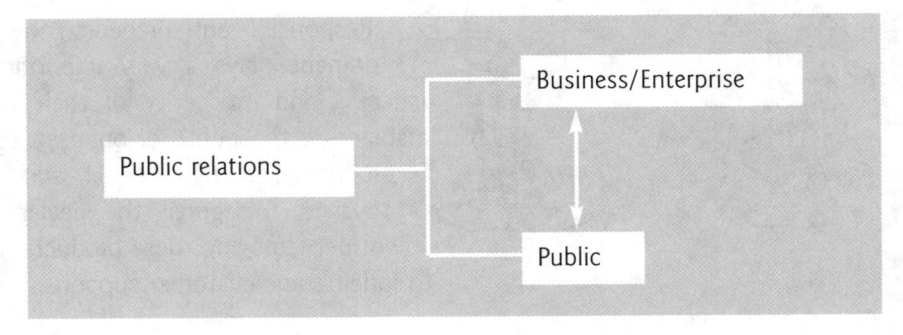

```
                              ┌── Business/Enterprise
        Public relations ─────┤           ↕
                              └── Public
```

The attitude, feelings and opinions of the public are affected by a wide variety of factors.

CHAPTER 8
The Public Relations Function

These factors include the following:
- The way in which the business employs and remunerates its staff;
- The attitude of the business towards the utilisation of resources;
- The replacement and conservation of resources;
- The quality and prices of the business's goods or services.

Because public relations is the most recent of the functions of a business, it is often confused with the marketing function.

What is the difference between these two functions?

Marketing is the function responsible for the **sale of the services or products** of the business, such as food, clothing or training (see Chapter 3).

With the help of public relations, the **business itself is marketed** or **'sold'**. This does not mean that the business itself is really sold, but that it is **promoted** to the public.

When we talk of public relations, a number of concepts are involved, such as:
- the image of the business;
- the attitude of the public towards the business;
- public relations;
- liaison (communication).

Many words are used to describe this function, and many different definitions also appear for this function in literature on the subject. We do not expect you to memorise all the definitions. It is more important to **understand** what such a definition means.

One of the definitions that contains most of these basic elements is:

Public relations involves a **deliberate, planned and sustained** process of **communication** to **establish and maintain mutual understanding** between the business and its environment.

THE ENTREPRENEURSHIP SERIES

Management for Entrepreneurs

The most important words in the definition are printed in bold. This should help you to compile your own definition, which you may find easier to understand and remember.

The basic elements of public relations will always be as follows:

- **Identify, understand and evaluate** the problem;
- Establish **who the public is**;
- Compile a **message** that is **clear and acceptable** to the public.

Figure 8.1

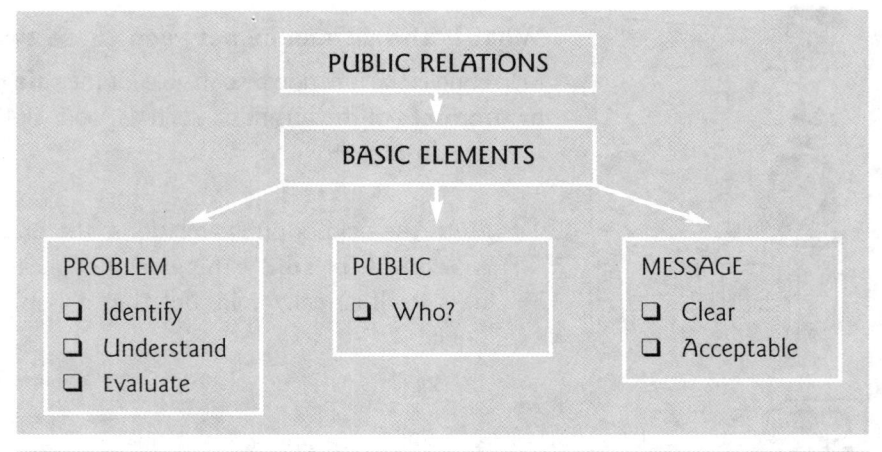

```
                    PUBLIC RELATIONS
                           ↓
                    BASIC ELEMENTS
              ↙            ↓            ↘
      PROBLEM           PUBLIC           MESSAGE
      ❏ Identify        ❏ Who?           ❏ Clear
      ❏ Understand                       ❏ Acceptable
      ❏ Evaluate
```

1. Compile your own definition of public relations, using the bold-printed words in the definition above.

   ....
   ....
   ....

2. What is the most important difference between the functions of public relations and marketing?

PUBLIC RELATIONS	MARKETING
....	....
....	....
....	....
....	....
....	....

CHAPTER 8
The Public Relations Function

4 OBJECTIVES OF PUBLIC RELATIONS

The main objective of public relations may be seen as a **process** that promotes and improves the image of the business among the public to establish a healthy relationship between the business and the public.

Figure 8.2

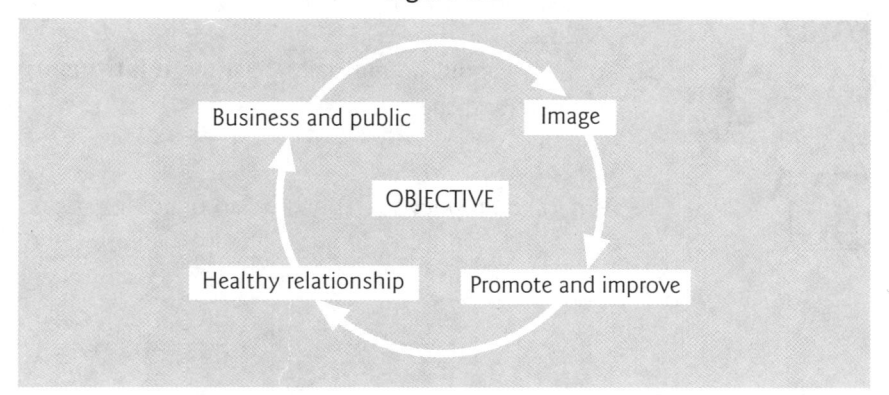

```
          Business and public  →  Image
                      OBJECTIVE
          Healthy relationship ← Promote and improve
```

Although public relations has a simple goal – **to create and maintain mutual knowledge and understanding in the business and among the public** – it fulfils a complex and important role.

It is naturally important to ensure that a good relationship (knowledge and understanding) is established between the business and the public. However, to ensure that the business succeeds and grows, this relationship must also succeed and grow. The relationship is therefore not just established, but must also be **maintained**.

In general we can say that the objectives of the public relations function can be deduced from the objectives of the business. In other words, **what** does the business aim to achieve?

As you know, the **primary objective** of any business is to make a **profit**. The achievement of this objective requires the support of various functions.

To support the primary objective of profit, therefore, each of the various functions in the business draws up certain **secondary objectives**.

THE ENTREPRENEURSHIP SERIES

Management for Entrepreneurs

The secondary objectives of public relations are as follows:
- To promote the **prosperity** of the business;
- To establish **goodwill** amongst the public;
- To make the business as a whole **acceptable** to employees and the public;
- To promote and improve the **image** of the business amongst the public;
- To bring about a mutually healthy **relationship** between the business and the public.

1. Why should public relations be an ongoing process?
   ....
   ....
   ....

2. Complete the diagram below by filling in the missing words.

```
                    OBJECTIVES
                   /          \
       ........... objective    Secondary objectives
       ❑ Profit                 ❑ Promote ...............
                                ❑ Establish .............
                                ❑ Make ..................
                                ❑ Improve ...............
                                ❑ Bring about ...........
```

5 INTEREST GROUPS

Who are the interest groups and the public to whom we refer?

These are the groups of people with whom the business must communicate for it to be successful.

When you decide to start your own business or to solve problems that arise within your business, it is necessary to identify those groups who are

CHAPTER 8
The Public Relations Function

affected or will be affected by what you intend to do. It is very important to **identify the public carefully, or you may overlook an important group**, which could cause problems for your business from the start.

For instance, because employers are dependent on the goodwill and support of their employees, they should note the provisions of the Department of Labour. This department represents the interests of all employees and administers the various Acts dealing with such matters, for instance:

- The Labour Relations Act 66 of 1995;
- The Occupational Health and Safety Act 85 of 1993;
- The Basic Conditions of Employment Act 75 of 1997.

The Department of Labour is therefore also an interest group in most businesses.

Other examples of typical interest groups are:

Employees:	Clerks, sales staff, workers, older and younger employees
Clientele:	Actual and potential customers and clients, regular and irregular customers and clients, suppliers and consumers
Media:	Local newspapers, magazines
The community:	Community leaders, inhabitants and trade unions

With the strong competition nowadays, businesses have a greater obligation than ever before towards the public. The public is more informed than before and will not stand for poor treatment, incorrect information or misunderstandings simply for the sake of loyalty towards a business.

Entrepreneurs therefore have a duty to keep their interest groups or potential customers informed so that they understand the intentions of the business. Entrepreneurs must also treat their interest groups fairly to build up a good relationship with them. In exchange, they will win a loyal public and will be able to rely on their support.

The public often chooses to identify with a business that has a stated policy on an issue, such as one that refuses to sell pornographic

THE ENTREPRENEURSHIP SERIES
Management for Entrepreneurs

magazines, rather than with one that makes no effort to establish good relations with consumers, employees and the community. For many businesses this means learning new social skills. For instance, they must take into account what the public expects from them, and decide whether their image and conduct is favourable enough to ensure success.

Healthy relations make the product or service more acceptable to the public, and can contribute to the financial success of the business.

An uninformed public, for instance, can be very negative towards the conversion of residential houses into office blocks. Reasons for their dissatisfaction may vary from the damage that will be done to the appearance of the area, to the increase in the number of businesses in an area. By providing more information on the positive aspects (such as job creation, the utilisation of empty stands or improvement in the appearance of a building), the public attitude can be changed, and this contributes to better relations.

The basis of good relations is often nothing more than good manners.

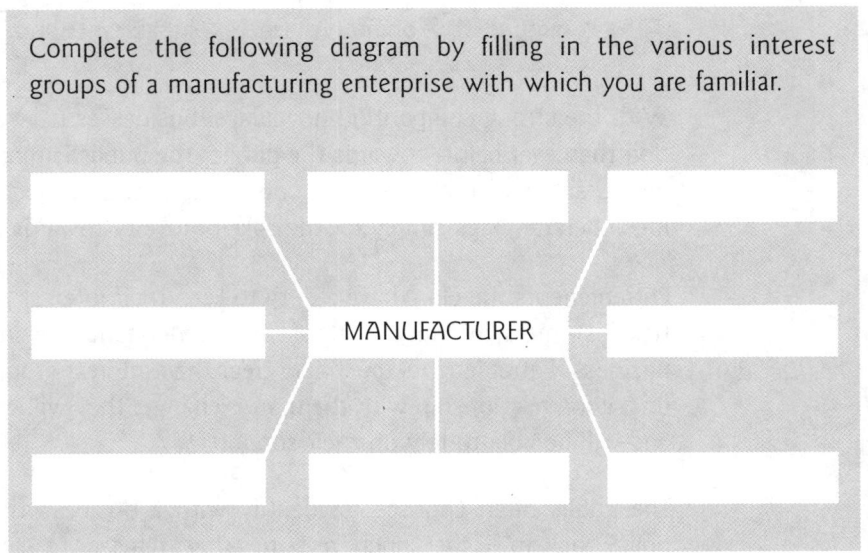

DO Complete the following diagram by filling in the various interest groups of a manufacturing enterprise with which you are familiar.

MANUFACTURER

CHAPTER 8
The Public Relations Function

8 SHAPING PUBLIC OPINION

When public opinion is formed, a certain image of the business is formed. However, people view a business in various ways. Everyone has her/his own opinion, and it is not always easy to convince people that they may perhaps have had the wrong impression of a certain matter.

For instance, we will look at the following answers that we got when we inquired about two businesses:

eg

What do you think of 'Yum-Yum Pies', which opened last month in this shopping centre?

Person A: I am very impressed – the pies are delicious!
Person B: I don't eat pies so I don't know.

How good is 'Binvin's Greengrocer'?

Person A: Well, the vegetables there are often old and wilted, and the owner is really grumpy.
Person B: If you want fresh flowers, you can always be certain of getting nice ones from old 'Binnie'.

We can see that there will be as many impressions of a business as there are people to have these impressions. Naturally, however, the ideal would be for everyone to have a good impression of a business.

However, a poor impression of a business does not disappear by being ignored. If a business has a poor image, it should look at ways of improving it. Even so, some dissatisfied clients may still be sceptical. However, satisfied clients who are aware of the advantages of the products or services of the business they support are the 'insurance policy' for the success and growth of any business.

What sort of image would a business like to have?

Every business should regard its image as an asset that requires constant development. This means that the owner or manager should constantly think of the image that the business conveys to the public.

In a smaller business, the manager or owner has the advantage of **direct contact** with interest groups and needs, and will with time know instinctively what the needs or her/his business's interest groups are.

The client's opinion is usually determined through **promotions**. In the case of domestic items or food, for instance, the **appearance of the shop** at which such items are bought, the **packaging** and naturally the **quality of the product** are all critical for public support of the business. For more expensive items such as cars, washing machines and computers, the user's opinion is often formed by the **after-sales service** offered by the various businesses.

A favourable image will determine whether:

- new staff would like to join the business;
- the business has an established and growing clientele;
- the media will give the business the benefit of the doubt in times of crisis.

How is public opinion usually formed?

Various factors affect the formation of public opinion. The following aspects are discussed briefly:

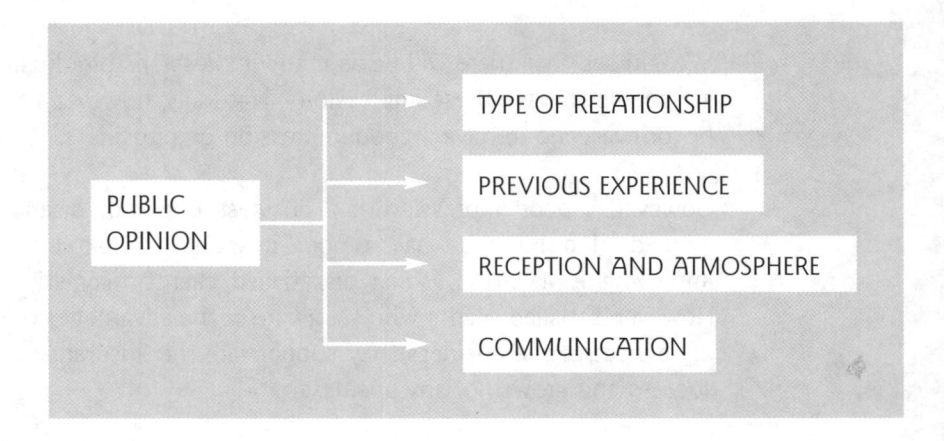

PUBLIC OPINION →
- TYPE OF RELATIONSHIP
- PREVIOUS EXPERIENCE
- RECEPTION AND ATMOSPHERE
- COMMUNICATION

CHAPTER 8
The Public Relations Function

The type of relationship
The type of relationship that interest groups have with the business will determine whether public opinion is favourable or not. For instance, when pieces of glass were found in Perrier mineral water, all consumers were warned, the product was withdrawn and clients were compensated. As a result, the image of the product was not damaged in any way.

Previous experience of specific transactions with the business
The most important advertisement for a business is when consumers share their experiences with one another. If consumers are satisfied with the service or product offered, and therefore have a good opinion of the business, they will tell other people. However, people tend to talk about negative experiences more than positive ones, so the opinion of others can also very easily be negatively affected.

Reception and atmosphere in the business
Although most businesses have a reception area, clients or customers are also received in other offices and in entertainment areas. All employees have contact to a greater or lesser extent with visitors and must therefore be informed about the way in which they should receive the public. The right behaviour is very important, because it affects the attitude of the public towards the business.

Naturally a neat entrance and a friendly reception will have a positive effect on any potential customer or client.

Communication
Communication by the business, such as telephone calls, letters or personal contact, is always a sign of what it really thinks of its clients.

Tips in this regard are:

Telephone technique	When a call is made or received and the contact is pleasant, both caller and receiver will react positively.
	Switchboard operators in particular must have good voice techniques that promote positive feelings, and must convey a positive image of the business.

THE ENTREPRENEURSHIP SERIES

Management for Entrepreneurs

☞	Letters and documents	All written communication with clients must be clear and correct and convey a positive image of the enterprise.
		Remember, when clients do not actually visit the business itself, written communication is probably the only way to remind them of it!
	Personal contact	Personal contact is very important in determining whether the business is successful or not. The following pointers may be useful: ❑ Know the public; ❑ Give customers a lot of attention; ❑ Treat everyone equally; ❑ Be helpful and friendly; ❑ Acknowledge mistakes made by the business; ❑ Apologise for mistakes and correct errors.

DO

1. Write down in approximately five lines what you understand by public opinion.

   ....
   ....
   ....
   ....
   ....

2. What effect does public opinion have on the image that a business projects?

   ....
   ....
   ....
   ....
   ....

CHAPTER 8
The Public Relations Function

1 METHODS OF COMMUNICATION

Public relations is a two-way process, consisting of the **sending** and **receiving** of messages. The business communicates with the public to introduce a new service or product, while from the public it receives feedback information in the form of suggestions, complaints and opinions.

Communication remains the most basic method of promotion for a business. Communication allows a business to identify, contact and persuade customers to purchase its products or services.

A smaller business enterprise will usually not be able to afford advertising on television or over the radio, and must therefore use other methods of promotion. The following are a few examples:

- ❑ **Networking**, where friends and acquaintances tell one another and others about the business.
- ❑ **Inviting journalists** from the local newspaper to the opening of the business.
- ❑ **Sending in an article or photographs** for publication if the press cannot be present at an important occasion, such as the release of a new product, the anniversary of the enterprise or a visit by important people.

It is very important to be creative when projecting an image, and you should consider using an assortment of methods to distinguish your business from similar businesses. Assume, for instance, that you have a home industry in a shopping complex containing another similar shop. To distinguish your shop from the other home industry, you could consider converting part of your shop into a coffee bar where customers can sit around small tables and enjoy coffee and a piece of cake. The appearance of the home industry can naturally also be used to attract the attention of prospective customers.

THE ENTREPRENEURSHIP SERIES
Management for Entrepreneurs

Example of an introduction

Elna Bernini started her business when she made her daughter Zizi's matric dance dress. One of Zizi's friends saw the dress and persuaded Elna to design another dress for her.

On the evening of the matric dance, the photographer from the local newspaper saw both girls and photographs of the two appeared the following week in the newspaper. Elna's name was inserted as designer of these special dresses, and the same day someone asked her to make a dress for one of the girls at a neighbouring school.

Of course, the news of someone making matric dance dresses spread like wildfire; this exchange of contacts is what is known as '**networking**'! Without Elna even needing to advertise, her beautiful dresses led to her business expanding so much that in a short space of time she was one of the candidates for 'businesswoman of the year'.

It is naturally also important to join **organisations** and **associations**, such as the local Chamber of Commerce, where networking can take place with people who have an interest in your business. In this way you can build up valuable **contacts**.

Explain the term 'networking' as it is used in the business world, and indicate how it can be used to benefit smaller businesses in particular.

....
....
....
....
....

8. SOCIAL RESPONSIBILITY

All entrepreneurs have a social responsibility towards the people responsible for their success – it is useful to follow the principle that in helping others, you help yourself. The responsibility is not limited only to the **environment** within which the business functions, but also includes **employees** of the business.

Employees

A good workforce is necessary to keep the business functioning. It is therefore important that the employer create the right sort of **supportive climate** in the business to satisfy employees' needs and to ensure that they perform as well as possible. One way in which you can do this is by granting financial study aid to children of employees, or to employees themselves. This will in turn contribute indirectly to improvement in work performance.

It is also important that the employer allow employees to participate in decision-making processes, give them training and allow them to acquire skills and motivation. Remember that staff who are well informed will generally be happier and more loyal than uninformed staff. They have greater enthusiasm for the objectives of the business for which they work because they understand that their personal success depends on the success of the business.

The environment

Most businesses in South Africa have begun to see that they can make an important contribution to better **social, ecological and aesthetic (attractive) environments**, which will be to the benefit not only of their employees, but also to the inhabitants of their area and to the country as a whole. These contributions include support for nature and environmental conservation activities, and anti-pollution campaigns.

When it comes to financial donations, it is usually a good idea to 'donate what you can afford'. Examples of donations are bursary allocations to employees' dependants, allocations to educational institutions, sponsorships or facilities made available to employees.

If a business fails to fulfil its social responsibilities or damages the environment, it will be regarded as a threat to society and will lose support.

A business remains dependent on the community for support. If entrepreneurs make promises which they later fail to fulfil, they can advertise as much as they want, but not much will change the poor image that they have created for themselves. However, the better the image of a business, the greater the support from the public will be.

> Explain the concept of 'social responsibility'.
> ....
> ....
> ....
> ....

9 SUMMARY

The role of public relations in the success and growth of any business, however large or small, cannot be underestimated. As you have seen from this chapter, the entrepreneur is dependent on people and their goodwill.

It is important to remember that public relations must not be confused with advertising or the marketing function. Marketing or advertising is concerned mainly with a particular product or service, while public relations is a process during which the business is made acceptable to the various interest groups. We can therefore say that this process 'sells' the business to the public.

10 SELF-EVALUATION

> 1. Write down the basic elements of the definition of public relations.
> ....
> ....
> ....

CHAPTER 8
The Public Relations Function

2. What is the difference between marketing and public relations?

MARKETING	PUBLIC RELATIONS
....	....
....	....
....	....
....	....
....	....

3. You have already done all the necessary preparations for starting your own business. Explain how you intend to promote your business to the public.

   ....
   ....
   ....
   ....
   ....

4. 'The function of public relations in a business has meaning only when the relationship between employer and employee is healthy and effective.' Discuss this statement.

   ....
   ....
   ....
   ....
   ....

5. What do you regard as the 'social responsibility' of a business?

   ....
   ....
   ....
   ....

11 REFERENCES

Bennett, R. 1989. *Small Business Survival*. London: Pitman.

Corke, A. 1985. *Effective Advertising and PR*. London: Pan Books.

Du Plessis, P.G. (ed.) 1993. *Toegepaste Bedryfsekonomie. 'n Inleidende Oorsig*. Pretoria: Haum.

Katz, B. 1991. *Turning Practical Communication into Business Power*. London: Mercury.

Le Roux, E.E. *et al.* 1995. *Ondernemingsbestuur. 'n Praktiese Benadering*. Johannesburg: Lexicon.

Resnik, P. 1988. *The Small Business Bible*. New York: Wiley.